Supercharged Quality

Supercharged Quality

Transform Passive Quality into Passionate Quality

MOHAN KARAMBELKAR

Foreword By
RALPH WATSON

PARTRIDGE
A Penguin Random House Company

ISBN:	Hardcover	978-1-4828-1641-9
	Softcover	978-1-4828-1642-6
	Ebook	978-1-4828-1643-3

To order additional copies of this book, contact
Partridge India
000 800 10062 62
www.partridgepublishing.com/india
orders.india@partridgepublishing.com

Contents

SECTION 1:
Drive for Quality

SECTION 2:
Set-up for Quality

SECTION 3:
Communication for Quality

SECTION 4:
Business and Quality

SECTION 5:
Maintaining quality

APPENDICES

To my father Late Dr Dattatreya Karambelkar,
who provided quality medical service in remote villages in
India with optimum use of limited resources

I

Foreword

By Ralph Watson

It is a sad truth that so many individuals and organisations pay lip service to this word 'quality' and do little to walk their talk. Much of the time, this is not due to any deliberate omission but rather to a lack of understanding and awareness. *Supercharged Quality* offers a fine and entertaining solution to that situation.

In creating this book, Mohan Karambelkar has walked his own talk on quality and has demonstrated his expertise and passion for the subject. He also brings to bear his skills and knowledge across a range of excellent tools, including Neuro-Linguistic Programming (NLP), which is highly appropriate in this application since it is about the study of excellence and that is what *Supercharged Quality* is about—quality excellence and how to achieve it. This excellent volume is well-written, balanced, informative, and easy to read. It offers instruction, tips, ideas, and models in equal measure alongside humour.

It has been a great pleasure and an eye-opener for me to read this book as my thirty-five years in business have taught me much about quality—including the good, the bad, and the ugly. I have learned mush in those years, and I'm delighted to say I have learned much from Mohan's fine work. If I have one regret, it is that the business world has had to wait until now to read it. If it were in my gift, I would make this book a compulsory reading. As it is, I am tempted to believe that Mohan Karambelkar is actually the secret identity of a new super hero on the mean streets of Business City. His name is Captain Quality.

Ralph Watson
International NLP Master Trainer

II

Preface

Let me start with a story. Once upon a time, a king decided to give a holy bath to the statue of God. The holy bath was given with milk. He ordered the people to contribute one litre of milk from each household, and the milk was to be deposited in the tank near the temple. One person thought that as other people are contributing the milk, it does not matter if he alone contributes water instead of milk. When the tank was opened, it was full of water as everybody thought the same thing—that somebody would contribute the milk. Quality often gets a similar fate. Organisations emphasise on quality being everyone's responsibility; however, in practice, it is seen as the responsibility of someone else. A marketing and sales person thinks that any lacuna in requirement will be taken care of by the design department. The design department person thinks that the production department will take care of any design error. The production person thinks that the testing team will sort the product and will not allow defective product to the customer. The testing team will think the service team is capable of handling issues in the field and so the product need not be tested thoroughly. Finally, the customer gets a poor quality product, and the organisation may lose the customer forever.

In the above case, quality management programme becomes a finger-pointing exercise. In reality, it should be effective so that everyone knows their responsibility and serves their customers (internal and external) well. This book looks at motivation for quality and how we can keep the motivation high for the quality programme.

Quality is often seen as a journey towards excellence. Quality professionals adopt statistical techniques and other methods and tools to achieve excellence (for example, Six Sigma is leading to perfection just a single error in million transactions/products).

Another school of thought is how successful people behave and how we can decode it so that their excellence can be reproduced. This is related Neuro-Linguistic Programming (NLP).

Since the highest intention for both is excellence, this book explores the commonality and works on how NLP can be used for quality management programme.

Most of the NLP concepts are taught as help for individuals. This book explores to apply them to an organisation. As per Company Law, company is a separate legal entity. We can treat as entity for NLP concepts also.

Most of the NLP concepts in this book are simple and will not need training in NLP. However, exercises of a therapeutic nature are to be conducted by a certified NLP practitioner only.

NLP is like an open-source software. There are many concepts and techniques applicable to management, education, life coaching, counselling, and many more. This book explores with reference to Quality Management. Each chapter introduces applicable concepts and explains in simple language such that even people without NLP knowledge can grasp the NLP concept.

If you are more curious about NLP, then the best thing is to attend NLP course. The NLP training levels are NLP Practitioner, NLP Master Practitioner, NLP Train the Trainer, and Master Trainer of NLP. I referred to almost all the levels while writing this book and did not put any restriction. As NLP Master Trainer, Dr David Lincoln says, 'If you start with practitioner level, you will develop interest in NLP, and you will go on doing higher levels to become NLP trainer'.

A focused mind is a powerful resource for the quality management programme. We can achieve a resourceful state (of mind) through Neuro-Linguistic Programming (NLP) and supercharge the quality management programme.

III

Superchargers

As the name indicates, this book is uncommon compared to the typical books on quality. Most of the books focus on a role of statistics in quality control or standards and audit against those standards or Total Quality Management (TQM) with change in culture. This book believes that if an unconscious mind plays an important role in an individual's success, it can play an equally important role in the organisational success. Neuro-Linguistic Programming deals with the power of the unconscious mind. This book explores various NLP concepts.

As shown in figure iii.i, business excellence can have three areas: product, process, and people. Product quality is linked with quality of design, quality plan, and quality control. Process quality is linked to quality of conformance, statistical process control, and quality assurance. People quality is considered as the domain of human resources management.

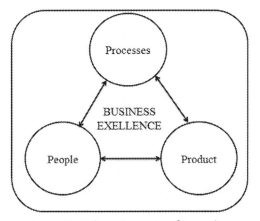

Figure iii.i Three Domains for quality

This book sees people from the NLP perspective and proposes quality management programme that interweaves quality concepts with NLP concepts. The structure of the book is shown in figure iii.ii.

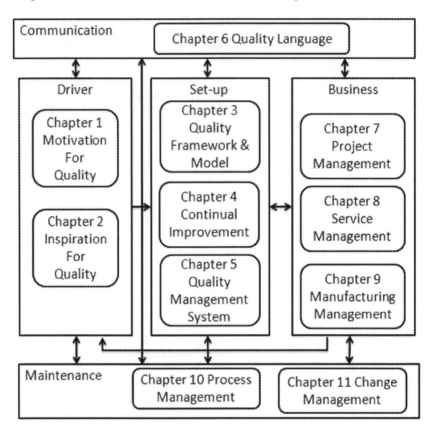

Figure iii.ii Structure of the book

'Driver' box shows the driving forces—motivation for quality and inspiration for quality. The first chapter explores the understanding of motivation for quality. The supercharger is a clear motivational strategy for quality management programme. The second chapter looks at the philosophy of Quality Gurus. The superchargers are an inspiration from Gurus and NLP presupposition.

'Set-up' box is about setting up the quality management programme. The third chapter puts together various quality models and frameworks. Supercharger is a selection of right processes or/and right model for quality management programme. The fourth chapter suggests adopting a continual improvement approach. The supercharger for continual improvement is utilisation of beliefs and behaviour. The fifth chapter describes how to build quality management system (QMS). Superchargers for QMS are neurological levels and a balanced approach.

'Communication' box is about the communication required. The sixth chapter gives quality language that organisations need to adopt. The learning and development team plays an important role in training people on QMS, continual improvement, and quality language. Trainings and coaching are covered in this chapter.

'Business' box indicates the major components of businesses. Businesses like constructions and infrastructure development focus primarily on project and project management. Businesses like transportation and hospitality have primary focus on services and service management. The third important component is manufacturing of products; quality aspects in manufacturing have been covered by various books on quality. Hence, this book will cover quality aspects in short. A business will have these three components at variable degree.

The seventh chapter covers project management. Superchargers for project management are NLP techniques like goal setting and visualisation. Eighth chapter discusses service management. Superchargers for service management are techniques for rapport building and strategies. The ninth chapter is about manufacturing management and supercharger is visualisation.

'Maintenance' box indicates the ongoing activities of quality management system. Chapter 10 addresses process management. Supercharger for process management is competency stages. Chapter 11 provides change management. Superchargers for change management are techniques to change beliefs. Though these processes are under maintenance, process management and change management begin as we start the set-up of QMS.

Business success propels the motivation further. It is a spiral of success. NLP tools are superchargers. When superchargers trigger, passive quality programme transforms into passionate quality programme.

If we consider NLP tools as objects of kaleidoscope, this book shows one pattern with reference to my model of the world (or quality management). If you turn around a bit, you can see another pattern and use NLP in your personal and professional lives in different ways.

IV

Acknowledgement

Being a Quality Assurance professional, I focused on implementing Quality standards and Quality frameworks in various organisations. For leadership and communication skills, I joined Toastmasters in 2005 in Singapore and later started clubs in Pune (India). At Toastmasters Club, Mr Ganesh Srinivasan introduced me to NLP, and my association started with NLP & HUNA group, Pune. I would like to thank Mr Ganesh Srinivasan.

I studied NLP courses at ANLP Goa. I am fully indebted to trainers Dr David Lincoln, Mr Ralph Watson, Sushil Mehrotra, and Umesh Soman.

I appreciate Dr David Lincoln for having given in-depth knowledge on NLP in a lucid manner and Mr Ralph Watson for having given business perspective of NLP and also coaching aspects. Their training and guidance encouraged me to bring out this book.

I would like to thank my IIT professors, Prof. M. N. Gopalan, for developing a scientific bend of mind, and Prof. A. Subhash Babu for practical approach.

I would like thank toastmasters clubs, especially ACCA Toastmasters Singapore, Toastmasters Club of Pune, and Eaton Toastmasters Club for leadership opportunities and for the feedback from fellow toastmasters.

I would like to thank Mr Manas Karambelkar for creatively adding pictures for this book. I would like to thank Mrs Supriya Karambelkar for checking the book from grammar and reading perspective.

I would like to thank Partridge team for giving final shape to this book.

Mohan Karambelkar

V

About the Author

Mohan Karambelkar has unique qualifications of being an engineer from IIT Mumbai (M.Tech. Reliability Engineering) and an accountant (qualified from ACCA, UK and CIMA, UK). He also has certifications CISA from ISACA (USA), CSQA from QAI (USA), and ITIL Expert from EXIN (The Netherlands). Mohan is an auditor for ISO 9001, ISO 20000, and ISO 27000. He is also Certified Test Analyst and Certified Test Manager from ISTQB. His twenty-four years of experience includes mainly quality management and software development. He has worked with IT department, engineering department, and accounting department. He is associated with ANLP India and is a Certified NLP Trainer. He is a member of toastmasters since September 2005 and achieved the highest title 'Distinguished Toastmaster'. Mohan owns Pune-based PQR Consultancy Services LLP; the firm provides consultancy for Productivity, Quality, and Reliability.

SECTION 1:

Drive for Quality

1

Motivation for Quality

Quality Management as a profession exists over a century. It started as an inspection job in mass production. Then it evolved into quality assurance through process control and use of statistical control. Later, quality became a part of every aspect of business and emerged as Total Quality Management. Evolution in quality profession progressed towards comprehensive coverage of business to excel in all areas.

The human race has shown a quest for quality. Human development moved the Stone Age to the Modern Age in stages, with quality improvements at every stage.

Pyramids were built 5,000 years back with great accuracy. That shows the quality in ancient period.

The aerospace industry today shows the high safety standards. This is a part of high-quality standards in today's world.

Every development indicates motivation for excellence and delivering a quality product. It is good to explore the motivation for quality in current situations.

This chapter looks at motivation for quality from NLP perspective. However, people have different perceptions of quality. This chapter explores the right strategy for motivation and having the right perception for quality management programme.

1.1 Prime Motivators—Power, Affiliation, and Achievement

David McCleland, a Harvard psychologist and an expert, says that people are motivated by one of the following three things:

- power and control
- affiliation and popularity
- achievement and success

As per perception filter (NLP Meta Programmes), people are motivated by two ways—first is achieving the target and second is avoiding the failure. A simple example could be students: students who wish to pass the exam (satisfaction with high marks) and students who do not wish to fail (satisfaction with minimal passing marks). It is good to understand the motivation of the organisation to implement the quality management system.

Power and control—away

Some organisations would like to have minimal quality management programme to survive in the market. Quality management is aimed at solving the problems and resolving crises. Quality is used to avoid or manage rejections or keeping the complaints at a minimum.

Power and control—towards

Some organisations would like to be market leaders by launching quality products and have control over the market. Quality management is aimed at producing high-quality products and services. Quality management gives a brand name for the organisation through high quality.

Affiliation and popularity—away

Some organisations would like to set up quality management system when people complain about lack of system.

Affiliation and popularity—towards

Some organisations would like to set up quality management system through which tools, processes, and trainings are established. In effect, it will ease operation for people, and people are also encouraged to improve the quality management system (QMS).

Achievement and success—away

Some organisations seek certifications because these are the minimum criteria to enter the market (export requirement or tender requirement)

Achievement and success—towards

Some organisations would like to achieve the certification through independent audits. They participate in quality award assessments and often achieve quality awards.

Let us explore more on motivation. Avoidance of failure is not a recipe for success, or fear of failure will not result in excellence. For example, a football or soccer team avoids loss and is satisfied with draw. In the league, the team will end up losing on goal difference. Excellence will come when the organisation looks for positive motivation that is towards. Motivation for 'away' will look for minimal things like minimum quality requirements, minimum passing criteria.

An organisation will have staff which will fall under all three or six categories. Quality programme should consider all three prime motivators:

- Quality Programme will take pride in delivering the best or top quality.
- Quality Programme will be helpful in learning as well as in day-to-day work.
- Quality Programme will have recognitions for achievement and will provide the opportunities for achievements.

1.2 Where to Park Negatives

Quality programme is focused on 'towards'. Negatives are weaknesses (internal) and threats (external). A realistic person will have balance of towards and away and a pessimist will focus on away. An organisation needs to deal with failures and rejection. From the NLP perspective, the approach is as follows:

- In case of failures of past, take all learning.
- In case of anxiety of future, consider risk management; develop risk mitigation and contingency plan.

Risk management is discussed in Appendix E.

1.3 Tony Robbins's Six Motivators

Famous NLP practitioner and motivational speaker Tony Robbins suggested six human needs which will be the motivators. Let us link with quality.

- *Significance*: When we do quality work, we will understand our importance and pat at the back. For example, if a person does the job of packaging electronic equipments, he will realise the significance of his job by understanding the possible consequences of poor packaging. He will be motivated because of the significance of the job. This is motivation for achievements.
- *Connection*: When we work together with a group or a team, we develop a bonding. This gives a sense of belongingness. The relationship makes us to respect each other. This is the motivation for affiliation and popularity. We understand that quality work needs collaboration and cooperation.
- *Contribution*: We often look at the larger picture and know we are part of the society or community. With an inherent nature of helping, we wish to contribute to the society. Organisations look for Corporate Social Responsibility so that individuals will be motivated and get the opportunity to contribute.
- *Growth*: We strive for growth—economic growth, knowledge growth, spiritual growth, and growth in many other areas. Business also understands that business will grow when community will grow, and community will grow when individuals will grow. Individual growth fuels the organisation growth. Growth is also a factor or a measure for quality.
- *Certainty*: We need predictability in life and in work. In case of a business, quality management system provides processes (how) and roles and responsibilities (who and what), which brings predictability in work; it satisfies the certainty needs.
- *Uncertainty*: We get bored when life is routine or certain; we would like to have challenges. In case of business, the business dynamics throw new quality challenges (problems). The problem-solving work satisfies our 'uncertainty' needs.

Quality Management System (QMS) considers that—

- Processes will be well defined and move towards higher maturity to bring certainty or predictability.
- Business environment is dynamics and that QMS needs detection of current challenges and future challenges and their corrective actions and preventive actions, that is, moving from uncertainty to certainty.
- QMS needs to monitor the growth.
- QMS needs mechanism to recognise achievements.
- QMS needs to look at the synergy levels or teamwork.
- QMS needs to consider bigger picture with vision and mission and consider the contribution to society.

1.4 Perceptions about Quality

People have some perception on quality, and they see/hear/feel/think that is the reality (NLP principle—perception is projection). These perceptions may be impressions based on the way they experienced quality management programme in their organisation. It is good to discuss these perceptions and in reality 'What is NOT Quality'.

- *Temporary change*: Some people think quality is a flavour of the month. Management will celebrate quality month every year, and things will fall back soon. This is a seasonal change. However, quality improvement requires permanent change to better method or process. Quality programme includes change management.
- *Corrective action*: Some people think good problem solving skills and quick corrective actions mean good quality. When a person resolves crises, the management treats that person as a hero and ignores the root causes of the crises. Quality programme focuses on preventive action and proactive approach.
- *Window dressing*: This term has been borrowed from finance. Quality reports are made to look nice and attractive. Management would like to see nice things, and secondly, employees are also afraid to report bad news. This gives a reason to push problems under the carpet. Finally, the problems become crises. Crises

solution brings heroism. Quality programme promotes true and fair reporting without fear. Quality programme encourages early detection and prevention.

- *Paper chase*: Organisations often are motivated by the various certifications. People focus so much on certifications' criteria that they attempt to fit the business into certification criteria and, sometimes, at the cost of productivity. Unnecessary activities are added as a part of compliance. For example, IT organisation was creating two sets of documentation—one for ISO 9001 and the other for CMMI. The certification frameworks are the means for quality improvements and not the ends. Hence, all certifications are thoroughly checked for business benefits.

- *One-time activity*: Some organisations are fascinated by quality awards—national and international. To win the award, the project team is set up, and resources are devoted towards winning the award. People equate quality with the award and think quality as a one-time activity. Once the award is achieved, the project team is dismantled, resources are taken off, and quality drive becomes a history. People do not consider quality as an ongoing activity.

- *Documentation*: Quality Management System (QMS) requires certain documentation. For example, process documents, records as part of evidence, and work instructions. People think quality means documentation. Good documentation is equated with good quality. People devote more time towards documentation and become less responsive towards actual work. Sometimes, documentation may be for the sake of documentation. Documentation is a supporting tool for quality. Documentation with purpose will be more meaningful. Documentation serves different purposes—training new staff, understanding the information flow, and implementing tool for processes.

- *Satisfying audits*: Quality is often driven by certifications; for example, ISO 9001, ISO 14000, ISO 20000, and ISO 27000 certifications. People face a number of audits and alerts on compliance to the various standards. People think that if the auditor finds nothing denoting non-compliance, then they are doing a quality job. In short, quality means satisfying the auditor. In reality, there are many stakeholders whose quality requirements are to be satisfied.

1.5 People Have Preferences

People will have preferences for their working style. People will be motivated when they have work that matches their working style. Quality Management System should not force to change their working style because every style has certain advantages and disadvantages.

Myers Briggs Type Indicator (MBTI) is one of the ways to understand people's preferences. There are sixteen different personality types based on four parameters (as shown in Figure 1.1).

	Sensing (S)		Intuitive (N)		
Introverted	ISTJ	ISFJ	INFJ	INTJ	Judging (J)
(I)	ISTP	ISFP	INFP	INTP	Perceiving
Extroverted	ESTP	ESFP	ENFP	ENTP	(P)
(E)	ESTJ	ESFJ	ENFJ	ENTJ	Judging (J)
	Thinking (T)	Feeling (F)	Thinking (T)		

Figure 1.1 MBTI—sixteen combinations

Each parameter has two options. Let us explore their link to quality.

- Favourite world or energy source: Two types of this sort are—

  • Introverted (**I**)—draws energy from inner world—information, thought, ideas, and other reflection. Requires 'private time' to recharge. Quality Improvement will come from creative ideas, and processes can be thorough when a thoughtful person works on them. Introvert can contribute through ideas and detailing.
  • Extraverted (**E**)—draws energy from outer world—people, places, and activities. Feels deprived if cut off from the interaction with outside world. Quality needs teamwork, and QMS need to be promoted among the people. Extrovert can contribute to promotion of quality through people orientation.

- Information: Two types of this sort are—

  • Sensing (**S**)—prefers clear and concrete data, information, and facts and figures and is comfortable with logic but dislikes fuzzy or ambiguous situations. Quality projects and reporting needs logical interpretation of facts and figures. Sensing people can help in reporting on Quality.

- Intuitive (N)—prefers imagination, patterns, big picture; is comfortable with ambiguity. Quality looks forwards to out-of-box solution. Intuitive people can give out-of-box solution through imagination.

– Decision making: Two types of this sort are—

- Thinking (T)—looks at the logic in decision and required tasks; accepts conflicts as natural. The processes in QMS are logical and optimised. Thinking person can contribute to the processes through decision making and resolution.
- Feeling (F)—considers feelings and impact on people; seeks consensus and popular opinion. Quality needs acceptance from people. Feeling person can understand the opinions and seeks the acceptance.

– Structure or day-to-day lifestyle: Two types of this sort are—

- Judging (J)—Plans and focuses on tasks; avoids stress due to deadlines. Quality planning is part of QMS. Judging person can contribute well in planning and check on the process compliance.
- Perceiving (P)—acts without plan, does multitasking, works best when close to deadline. Perceiving person can handle emergency and high-priority incidents and can thus contribute to quality resolution.

Thus, an organisation needs different types of people to excel in quality.

1.6 Other Preferences of People

Meta programme (Refer Appendix A and Appendix C) gives the preferences of people. We can discuss different polarities.

Two polarities can be someone procedure-oriented (procedure type) and the other with freedom to have his/her own method (option type).

A procedure-type person will look for processes or methods or work instructions and will be happy about QMS as it provides the procedure (satisfying Certainty need). An option-type person will be happy to explore new things, and he or she may consider QMS as bureaucracy. He or she will be motivated to work on process improvements or problem-solving work.

Another polarity is about judging their quality of work. The two polarities are: internal, who are their own judge, and external, who check with others or check with the support of facts and figures. From a quality perspective, we encourage data-based decision or fact-based decision. As part of quality processes, work will be audited by an auditor or the product will be tested. An external person will easily accept audits and would like to provide the facts and figures. They are motivated with good report from external sources like auditors. An internal person has his or her own standards. He or she will not accept the quality processes easily. The challenge is to check whether their own standards match quality management system standards. These people (Internal oriented) should be involved in development of quality management system standards.

1.7 Quality Is Embedded

Nowadays, every business is Information Technology (IT) business because every aspect of business uses information technology, and we can see hardware and software. Similar to IT, quality needs presence in every aspect of business—work, product, and service. However, lack of quality gets noticed more evidently if it is missing.

I would like to share Birbal's story to illustrate that quality should always be in a person's mind. The story goes as follows:

Once, Emperor Akbar received three identical statuettes from a neighbouring king who asked him to rate them as good, better, and best. The courtiers could not find the difference. Finally, it was Birbal's turn. Birbal observed the statuettes carefully. He found a small hole in the right ear. Birbal took a small metal piece and inserted it in the right ear. For the first statuette, it came out of the left ear. For the second statuette, it came out of the mouth, and for the third statuette, it became a part of the statuette as it did not come out.

Birbal graded first statuette as good, second as better, and third as best. Akbar's courtiers could not understand the rating. Then Birbal explained that the statuettes were similar to people. The first type listens about quality and forgets. The second listens and talks about quality, but it is lip service and is not performing. For the third type, quality becomes part of them; they are quality conscious. Hence, these people are graded as best.

Quality needs to be embedded in the work, product, and service. This happens when we have motivation and skill. Motivation brings awareness, and skills provide competence. A person will acquire skills when he or she is motivated.

1.8 Quality Check by an Unconscious Mind

One of the prime directives of an unconscious mind is to support the morality you were taught and accepted. When we do our work, a question will pop in our mind: 'Is it right?' Our unconscious mind will give the answer based on our moral values.

There is a story of a sculptor. The sculptor was working on a huge idol of a goddess that he was making for the local temple, when a young man walked into his workshop. As the young man marvelled at the idol, he suddenly noticed another idol, almost identical, lying on the ground. 'Do you need two of these?' he asked. 'No' came the reply. 'We only need one. But the first one got damaged in the finishing stages. Hence, I am doing it again.'

The young man looked closely at the idol on the ground. It looked perfect. He could not see any signs of damage. 'Where is the flaw?' he asked. 'Look carefully,' said the sculptor, 'and you will notice a scratch under the left eye.' 'Wait a minute!' said the young man. 'Where will this idol be installed?'

The sculptor explained that it would be on a platform fifteen feet high inside the temple. And the young man quickly retorted, 'At that distance, who will know there is a scratch beneath the eye?' The sculptor smiled and said, 'I will'.

1.9 Quality Strategy

Successful teams and successful organisations have one thing in common. It is high level of motivation. Organisation leaders need to have strategy for motivating people for quality. The reward and recognition are to be integrated with quality job or quality performance.

- As an organisation leader, one should set the example of commitment to the quality. Quality commitment flows downwards and across the whole organisation.
- An organisation should set the values that will guide on quality work (Section 1.7 and 1.8. More discussion on values is in Chapter 5).
- An organisation should provide meaningful work, timely recognition, and reward matching the achievement.
- An organisation should eliminate demotivators and misconception through positive communication and transparent reward and recognition system.

1.10 In Summary

Quality programme needs tools, processes, and people. Tools can be procured, and processes can be developed with the help of process experts and are also available with quality models. The success of quality programme depends on people and their motivation for quality.

Motivation for quality varies from person to person. People have preferences; it is the alignment of their preference to quality that will provide meaningful work for the people. Quality programme should have a strategy for motivation.

People will have perception about quality based on their experiences. Those perceptions may not be the right motivation. Quality programme will have strategy for motivating people for quality.

Strategies are towards (attaining maximum) or away (achieving minimal). Towards strategy will work better.

2

Quality Gurus

Isaac Newton said, 'If I have seen further, it is by standing on the shoulders of giants'. If we wish to work on quality management system, it is good to look at the works of Quality Gurus. They are the inspiration for quality professionals as well as business persons.

This chapter provides a brief introduction of Quality Gurus and their approach to quality management.

2.1 W. Edwards Deming

Deming made a significant impact on quality profession through his philosophy and application of statistical quality control. From 1950 (after World War II), he worked with Japanese industry to provide training on statistical quality control. This led to the success of Japan as a manufacturer of innovative high-quality products. This contributed significantly towards Japan becoming an economic power.

In 1980, he made a great impact on the United States when he delivered the broadcast *If Japan Can . . . Why Can't We* and through his book, *Out of Crisis*. He summed his message with fourteen points and seven deadly sins.

Deming gave fourteen points, which are as follows:

1. *Create constancy of purpose for improvement of product and services.* This is about vision, mission, and long-term plans. Short-term solution (reactive approach or fire fighting) will not work in the long run.
2. *Adopt the new philosophy* (of customer-driven continuous improvement). Instead of reacting to competitive pressure,

consider customers' needs and embrace quality management across the organisation to meet the customers' needs.

3. *Cease dependence on mass inspection.* Inspections only find the defect and not prevent them. Hence, inspection approach is costly and unreliable. Process approach with statistical control will align with new philosophy (point 2).

4. *End the practice of awarding business on price tag alone.* An organisation should consider suppliers as its partners in quality. Suppliers shouldn't compete for the business based on price alone (at the cost of quality). Multiple suppliers will add to variation in processes and inconsistency in quality. It is good to have a single source of supply for any one item.

5. *Constantly and forever improve the systems of production and services.* This is about Plan-Do-Check-Act (PDCA cycle—It is discussed in Chapter 4) or Kaizen (Japanese term for continual improvements).

6. *Use training on the job.* It is about the development of modern training, covering process variation, teamwork, and quality philosophy. This is in addition to technical skills training.

7. *Teach and institute leadership.* Leadership means being a coach who can provide resources and support. A leader should focus on realising the potential of subordinates and not managing numbers and targets.

8. *Drive out fear and create trust.* This is to express ideas or issues fearlessly. Subordinates should feel valued and motivated to perform quality job.

9. *Break down barriers between departments.* This is to optimise work of individuals and teams through collaboration and consensus. It is also about shared vision and cross-functional teams for improvement.

10. *Get rid of unclear slogans and posters.* Leaders/managers often give nicely worded slogans without actions. Leaders should walk the talk.

11. *Eliminate management by objective.* Number-driven production will provide number only and not quality. There can be productivity at the cost of quality. However, productivity with process improvement can lead to good quality.

12. *Remove barriers that stand between the hourly worker and his right to pride of workmanship.* Competition with monetary rewards

will not improve quality. System improvement will bring improvement in everyone.

13. *Implement education and self-improvement.* This is about lifelong learning and continual improvement. An organisation should institute a vigorous programme of education and training for everyone.

14. *Take action and make transformation for everyone.* This is to create a structure in top management that will push every day on the above thirteen points.

There are no steps. Quality initiative needs to have a plan to implement these fourteen points.

2.2 Joseph M. Juran

Juran made a significant impact on quality through his books on quality, especially *Juran's Quality Control Handbook.* This handbook is considered as the quality bible. He is well known for Pareto principle (80:20 rule), Cost of Quality, and Trilogy that is, cross-functional approach.

Juran's trilogy is as follows:

Quality Planning

- Establish quality goals (long-term, short-term) and prioritise them.
- Identify external customers as well as internal customers.
- Identify customers' needs
- Translate the needs into specification (our language).
- Design, develop, and optimise the products and services that meet specifications and quality goals.
- Track performance.

Quality Control

- Identify the elements that need to be controlled.
- Establish measurement process and performance standard.
- Measure actual performance and identify the differences.
- Act on differences by taking corrective and/or preventive action.

Quality Improvements

- Identify opportunities for improvement.
- Get management commitment.
- Get support from workforce and get workforce involved.
- Provide appropriate training.
- Maintain and sustain improvements.

Juran has suggested taking up projects for quality improvements.

2.3 Philip Crosby

Philip Crosby is well known for introducing maturity levels that are now used in IT by Capability and Maturity Model Integrated (CMMI) and Control Objective IT Related Technology (COBIT). He is also known for Zero Defect programme (ZD) and Do It Right the First Time (DRIFT) and has several books to his name.

Crosby gave fourteen steps for quality programme, which are as follows:

1. Make it clear that management is committed to quality. Quality should get visibility at the management level.
2. Form quality improvement teams with representatives from each department. This will make a cross-functional/departmental team with ability to take actions in the department.
3. Determine where current and potential quality problems lie. This can be based on various sources, for example, rework, delays, and customer complaints.
4. Evaluate the cost of quality and explain its use as a management tool. This will show how quality programme will be profitable.
5. Raise the quality awareness and personal concern of all employees. This is to communicate outcome of the previous four steps. Employees will be aware of the significance of quality improvement programme.
6. Take actions to correct problems identified through the previous steps. This is to find solution to the problems identified earlier (in Step 3).
7. Establish a committee for the zero-defects programme. This is subset of quality improvement team. The committee members are

selected on ad hoc basis. The zero-defects programme is based on 'doing it right the first time' (DRIFT) and is not a motivational programme or flavour of the month.

8. Train supervisors to carry out their part of the quality improvement programme actively. All managers will have sound understanding of the programme and will be fully aware of its value.

9. Hold a 'zero defects day' to let all employees realise that there has been a change. Managers will inform the employees. They will understand the significance of the new attitude.

10. Encourage all individuals to establish improvement goals for themselves and their groups. Employee will have short-term (one to three months) specific and measurable goals.

11. Encourage employees to communicate to management the obstacles they face in attaining their improvement goals. Finding the solution for obstacles is the main part of this step.

12. Recognise and appreciate those who participate. This is the programme to appreciate the performers who are outstanding.

13. Establish quality councils to communicate on a regular basis. The quality council is made up of quality professionals and team leaders to monitor the progress.

14. Do it all over again to emphasise that the quality improvement programme never ends. Repeating the programme makes it perpetual or ongoing.

2.4 Other Quality Gurus

Other quality gurus are Walter W. Shewhart, Kaoru Ishikawa, and Armanda Feigenbam. Walter W. Shewhart is the father of statistical quality control. He developed control charts and derived the statistical inference. Kaoru Ishikawa is best known for cause and effect diagram (also known as Ishikawa diagram). He also contributed towards quality concepts of internal customer, quality circles, and shared vision. Armanda Feigenbam promoted Total Quality Control, which later became Total Quality Management (TQM).

2.5 NLP Guru

NLP has a short history of forty years (since 1970s). However, it has roots from earlier concept by various psychologists. The NLP books and courses can provide the details. The NLP pioneers had a significant contribution, which is briefly mentioned as follows:

Richard Bandler and John Grinder

Richard Bandler and John Grinder are the founders of NLP. In 1972, Richard Bandler was a psychology student at University of California, and John Grinder was an assistant professor in the linguistics faculty at the University of California. Both took up activity of behavioural modelling by combining Grinder's linguistic skills and Bandler's creative modelling skills. Experiment was to understand the patterns behind the success. They wrote several books together—*The Structure of Magic*, Volumes I and II, *Frogs into Princes*, *Trance-Formation*, and *Reframing: Neuro-Linguistic Programming and the Transformation of Meaning*.

Virginia Satir

Bandler and Grinder studied her and developed Meta Model in NLP. She also developed model of four personality types—the blamer, placatory, distracter, and computer.

Milton Erickson

Milton Erickson introduced the therapeutic use of hypnosis with clever application of ambiguous language. His language pattern forms Milton model.

Other NLP pioneers

Robert Dilts, Judith DeLozier, Leslie Cameron, and David Gordon joined NLP development. Robert Dilts has contributed in the area of beliefs and strategies. Judith DeLozier worked on modelling projects with Robert Dilts. Leslie Cameron and David Gordon are authors and co-developers of NLP.

2.6 NLP Aspects

Key points in Quality philosophies of different Quality Gurus are

- Purpose and goal setting with reference to quality
- Forming team or council for quality
- Communication for quality

NLP will be useful in all these three areas.

There are NLP presuppositions which are useful for quality management.

- *If what you are doing is not working, do something else.* This is to explore new options and look for improvement. It is incorrect to expect different results from continuing to do the same steps. This is a useful assumption for continual improvement.
- *Everyone is in charge of their mind and, therefore, their results.* Our mind is a key resource for producing result. The result will depend on how we control our thoughts or mind. For achieving quality, awareness of this presupposition is necessary. This brings accountability for quality in everyone.
- *People work perfectly to produce the results they are getting.* This is to question whether people are imperfect or systems are imperfect. With this presupposition, we will focus on system improvements and move away from blaming people. Another important aspect is forgiveness. We need to practice—'To err is human, to forgive is divine and to perfect the system is pragmatism'.
- *There is no such thing as failure, only feedback.* The most important part of failure is the learning and inputs for system improvements. This will contribute towards doing things differently.
- *Positive change always comes from adding resources.* These are the resources for the mind that can do quality job. The resources for mind are the positive states of mind. This goes very well with Deming's point, 'Drive out fear and create trust'.

The presuppositions of NLP are like codes of conduct and convenient beliefs for results. The list of all NLP presuppositions is given in

Appendix B. Each presupposition can provoke thoughts which will be useful for implementing quality improvements.

2.7 In Summary

Quality Gurus are the people who walk the talk. Their philosophies will form the guidelines for the quality programme for the organisation. Quality managers can look at them as role models and drive successful quality programme.

SECTION 2:

Set-up for Quality

3

Quality Models and Frameworks

Several models and frameworks for quality management have cropped up in the last few decades. Models galore have often caused confusion on selection and implementation. Two polarities can be this: an organisation wishes to implement all models (or maximum number of models), and an organisation thinks none of the model is suitable for them. This chapter will look into different models.

It is important to understand that we will utilise models for the business and will not fit business into model. In other words, model should bring effectiveness, efficiency, and energy to the business and not consume (net) efficiency, effectiveness, and energy from the business.

The chapter will briefly introduce models and will provide guidelines on selection. The details on models and methodologies are available in books on quality. Some of the models are from Information Technology domain. However, these are good for learning quality concepts.

3.1 ISO 9000 QMS Standard

This came into existence in 1987 and had a major revision in 2000. It made a way for third-party audit to certify organisation for compliance to this standard. The increase in certified organisation in all parts of the world shows its popularity. Figure 3.1 shows the process-based model for quality management system.

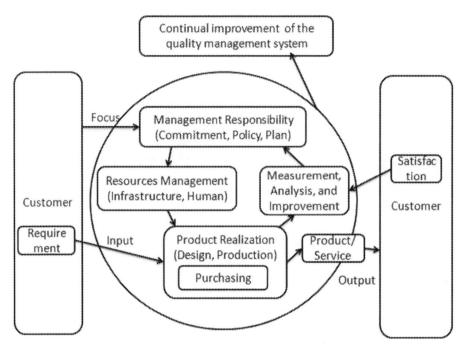

Figure 3.1 ISO 9001 QMS model

Model has adopted 'Plan-DO-Check-Act' (PDCA) to implement continual improvement. The standard advocates eight principles related to eight areas that are customer focus, leadership, involvement of people, process approach, system approach, continual improvement, factual approach to decision making, and mutually beneficial supplier relationship.

The documented quality management system is sometimes viewed as document for the sake of standards, and some people wonder about the link between product quality and standard. Finally, it is up to the organisation to decide how to implement it and how benefits are reaped.

3.2 Malcom Baldridge National Quality Award (MBNQA)

This award was conferred for the first time in 1988, and since then, close to 100 companies became the award winners till 2012 in different award categories. The award has seven areas or aspects, and each has subcategories. Each area has certain points for rating, and the total points are 1,000. The model is reviewed regularly, and the changes may happen in subcategories and their points from year to year. The seven areas are as follows:

- Leadership [125]—(Organisational leadership [85], public responsibility and citizenship [40])
- Strategic planning [85]—(Strategy development [40], Strategy deployment [45])
- Customer focus [85]—(Customer and market knowledge [40], Customer satisfaction and relationship [45])
- Information and analysis [85]—(Measurement and organisational performance [40], Analysis of organisational performance [45])
- Human resources focus [85]—(Work system [35], Employee education, training and development [25], Employee well-being and satisfaction [25])
- Process management [85]—(Product and service process [55], Support process [15], Supplier and partnering process [15])
- Business results [450]—(Customer-focused result [115], Financial and market results [115], Human resources results [80], Supplier and partner result [25], Organisational effectiveness results [115])

This is a very comprehensive customer-centric model with focus on results. This has been adopted by others. For example, Australian Quality Award, Singapore Quality Award, and Canadian Quality Awards are almost the same. European quality model is also similar. Tata group in India also used MBNQA for their quality programme.

3.3 Deming Award

This award was given in 1952. This differs from MBNQA as it focuses more on processes and Total Quality Management (TQM), and gives less importance to the results. It has the following ten areas with equal importance:

- Policies
- Organisation
- Information
- Standardisation
- Human resources

- Quality assurance
- Maintenance
- Improvement
- Effects
- Future plans

Deming prize does not provide a model. However, ten criteria are critically examined. Hence, it is rated as the highest award or considered as a gold standard.

3.4 Six Sigma

This is a methodology developed by Motorola in 1985. General Electric used 'Six Sigma' as a business strategy in 1995, implemented it across the organisation, and saved billions of dollars. The benefits reaped were amazing. This is a project centric and based on statistical analysis of process variation. The certifications in Six Sigma are at individual level.

For improving existing processes, the methodology is DMAIC (Define problem or goal, Measure performance with understanding of variation, Analyse opportunities by detecting causes of variation, Improve performance through appropriate solution, and Control by establishing control system). For product development process, there is DFSS (Design for Six Sigma).

Since it is generic methodology, it can be applicable to manufacturing as well as services.

3.5 Capability and Maturity Model Integrated (CMMI)

It started as CMM a model for software development in 1991. In 2010, version 1.3 was released with three models: CMMI for development, CMMI for services, and CMMI for acquisition. It became comprehensive with addition of services and acquisition. The assessment for CMMI is known as SCAMPI and will indicate the maturity level.

Levels	Processes			
Level 5 Optimizing			Organizational Performance Management (OPM)	Causal Analysis and Resolution (CAR)
Level 4 Quantitatively Managed		Quantitative Project Management (QPM)	Organizational Process Performance (OPP)	
Level 3 Defined	Technical Solution (TS) Product Integration (PI) Requirement Development (RD) Validation (VAL) Verification (VER)	Integrated Project Management (IPM) Risk Management (RSKM)	Organizational Process Definition (OPD) Organizational Training (OT) Organizational Process Focus (OPF)	Decision Analysis & Resolution (DAR)
Level 2 Managed	Requirement Management (REQM)	Project Monitoring and Control (PMC) Project Planning (PP) Supplier Agreement Management (SAM)		Configuration Management (CM) Measurement and Analysis (MA) Process and Product Quality Assurance (PPQA)
Level 1 Initial				
	Engineering	*Project Management*	*Process Management*	*Support*
	Categories			

Figure 3.2 CMMI for development(stage presentation)

The implementation of CMMI or improvements can be either using stage representation or continuous representation. The continuous representation is linked to capability levels and stage representation is linked to maturity level. Figure 3.2 shows the CMMI processes for stage representation. This model is popular among the software companies, and leading software companies have achieved maturity level 5.

3.6 ITIL and ISO 20000

IT Infrastructure Library (ITIL) started in UK by compiling best practices in IT service Management. Version 1 was released in 1989, and Version 2 was released in 2001. ISO 20000, standard for certification for IT Service Management, was released in 2005 and revised in 2011.

ITIL version 3 was released in 2007. It has focused on service management processes for service strategy, service design, service transition, and service operation. The continual service improvement is across all the four phases of service management. Figure 3.3 shows the processes of ITIL version 3.

With the web technology, IT system started operating 24 × 7. Availability of the system and response time led to the need for good IT service management. ITIL provides an excellent IT infrastructure management model for quality service.

Service Life Cycle: ITIL

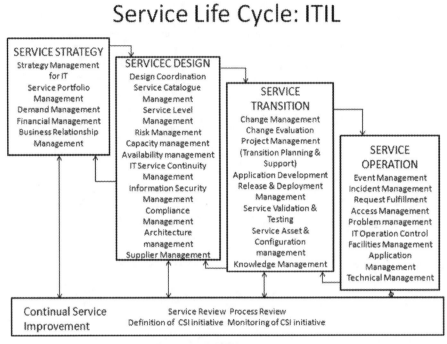

Figure 3.3 ITIL processes

3.7 Personal Software Processes (PSP) and Team Software Process (TSP)

Stephen Covey, in his book *The 7 Habits of Highly Effective People*, mentions the private victory focusing on self and public victory focusing on interaction with others. PSP and TSP is on similar line for software development team/organisation. Developer has certain tasks that are performed independently. PSP focuses on those processes of independent tasks. Personal excellence can come from effective defect management and time/task management. Team excellence can come from the collaboration built through TSP.

PSP and TSP is excellent model for quality management in software development. However, unlike CMMI/ISO 9000, there are no assessments for maturity or certification or award. Hence, it is purely the organisation's choice for quality improvements and not much on marketing strategy.

3.8 Control Objective Information-Related Technologies (COBIT)

COBIT was released for the first time in 1996 with target audience, mainly auditors performing IT audits. As IT became a significant part of business and more web-based applications are in use, COBIT version 5 released in 2012 is very comprehensive. COBIT also uses process maturity concept. This provides assurance on IT governance. This comprehensive model has the following processes:

- Governance of Enterprise IT

  o Evaluate, Direct, and Monitor

    - Ensure Governance Framework Setting and Maintenance
    - Ensure Benefits Delivery
    - Ensure Risk Optimisation
    - Ensure Resource Optimisation
    - Ensure Stakeholder Transparency

- Management of Enterprise IT

  o Align, Plan, and Organise

    - Manage the IT Management Framework
    - Manage Strategy
    - Manage Enterprise Architecture
    - Manage Innovation
    - Manage Portfolio
    - Manage Budget and Costs
    - Manage Human Resources
    - Manage Relationships

- Manage Service Agreements
- Manage Suppliers
- Manage Quality
- Manage Risk
- Manage Security

o Build, Acquire, and Implement

- Manage Programmes and Projects
- Manage Requirements Definition
- Manage Solutions, Identification, and Build
- Manage Availability and Capacity
- Manage Organisational Change Enablement
- Manage Changes
- Manage Change Acceptance and Transitioning
- Manage Knowledge
- Manage Assets
- Manage Configuration

o Deliver, Service, and Support

- Manage Operations
- Manage Service Requests and Incidents
- Manage Problems
- Manage Continuity
- Manage Security Services
- Manage Business Process Control

o Monitor, Evaluate, and Assess

- Monitor, Evaluate, and Assess Performance and Conformance
- Monitor, Evaluate, and Assess the System of Internal Control
- Monitor, Evaluate, and Assess Compliance With External Requirements

COBIT 5 has people aspects like managing relationship. COBIT 5 has two other important aspects:

- Principles

    o Meeting stakeholders' needs
    o Covering enterprise end-to-end
    o Applying single integrated framework
    o Enabling a holistic approach
    o Separating governance from management

- Enablers

    o Principles, policies, and framework
    o Processes
    o Organisational structure
    o Culture, ethics, and behaviour
    o Information
    o Services, infrastructure, and applications
    o People, skills, and competencies

3.9 Balanced Scorecard (BSC)

Though this is not a model and is a scorecard to measure, it has been extensively used in various models and frameworks; for example, explicitly in COBIT, MBNQA and also implicitly in ISO 9001.

What gets measured gets managed. Monitoring financial results alone will not give a clear picture of the business. The balanced scorecard gives a balanced approach by adding lead indicators for customer satisfaction, process, and learning and growth to financial measure. The combined measures provide the strategy tool when integrated with vision and mission.

3.10 Japanese Quality Management

Japanese manufacturing became known for quality in the 1970s. Toyota production system is well known as world class. Some of the terms in Japanese became equally popular. Some of the terms are as follows:

Kaizen

Kai means change and zen means good. Kaizen is Japanese term for continual improvement. Every employee contributes ideas for improvement. This is a big umbrella of quality movement, which covers several quality activities like quality circles, suggestion scheme, 5S (Sort, Set in Order, Shine, Standardise, Sustain/Systemise), just-in-time delivery (Pull production) and so on. All activities are supported with training, materials, and supervision that are needed for employees to achieve the higher standards.

Poka Yoke

Poka means mistake and yoke means avoiding. Poka Yoke is Japanese term for mistake proofing or defect prevention. The principles or methods of Poka Yoke are elimination, replacement, prevention, facilitation, detection, and mitigation.

5S (methodology)

This is about organising workplace to improve effectiveness and efficiency. All five words start with the letter 'S'—Seiri (Sort based on usefulness), Seiton (Straighten—to arrange properly for easy reach), Seiso (Shine—clean and tidy workplace), Seiketsu (Standardise to have uniform operation), and Shitsuke (Sustain through commitment).

Other Japanese terms

Heijunka is Japanese term for production levelling or smoothing. This is to minimise the fluctuation. Kaikaku is Japanese term for radical changes. This is done through projects. Jidoka is Japanese term for intelligent automation or automation with a human touch.

3.11 The McKinsey 7S Model

In the early '80s, Tom Peters and Robert Waterman, consultants at McKinsey (well known for book *In Search of Excellence*), developed this model. This is a generic model to improve performance of the organisation.

The 7S are divided into two groups—hard elements and soft elements. These elements are as follows:

- Hard elements: These elements are easy to define and ones the leader can influence.

  o Strategy: This is a long-term plan (of organisation) that sets the direction, builds a competitive advantage, and gives unique value proposition.
  o Structure: This is the organisational structure that sets the responsibilities and reporting and caters different functions of business.
  o System: This includes all the formal and informal processes and procedures that set the standards for doing the day-to-day activities and cover planning, executing, and monitoring.

- Soft elements: These elements are not easy to define, and culture has influence over these elements.

  - Skills: These are capabilities and competences of the employees of the organisation that gives the organisation distinctive advantage.
  - Style: It is the leadership approach of the top management and operational approach of the staff reflected in interaction and forms the culture of the organisation.
  - Staff: This is related to employees—how they are recruited, trained, motivated, and developed to perform their work in the organisation.
  - Shared value: This is at the centre stage of the model, often described as 'Super-ordinate goals'. The shared values guide staff towards work ethics and valued behaviour.

The important aspect of the model is that all 7S must be aligned with smooth interaction (as shown in Figure 3.4).

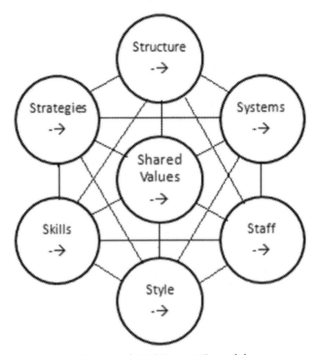

Figure 3.4 McKinsey 7S model

3.12 Model Selection

There are many models and frameworks. As per NLP presupposition, it is good to have choices than having no choice. Earlier IT companies used to have ISO 9001 certification for overall business, CMMI for software development, and ITIL/ISO 20000 certification for IT infrastructure management. It is questionable to have a number of certifications and its administration. It is necessary to have proper assessment to select model or models for quality programme. Some organisations focus on processes and refer models for those specific processes.

3.12.1 Business case

Traditionally, we prepare business case for any initiative taken in the organisation. Purpose of business case is to sell the project. Business will focus on financial numbers (cost and benefits) and non-financial or intangible benefits. A typical business case will have the following details:

- Brief description of the project
- Stakeholders (sponsor, project team, project manager, beneficiaries, people impacted)
- Alignment with corporate plan
- Benefits—this is tricky because of quantifying the indirect and intangible benefits.

  o Tangible: Revenue generated, defect reduction, cycle time reduction, cost reductions
  o Intangible: Better customer relationship, improved employee satisfaction or higher staff moral, reduced employee turnover, better control over assets, better predictability, reduced risk

- Cost—Resources required, training required
- Cost benefit analysis, return on investment
- Assumption
- Risks and contingencies
- Recommendation

3.12.2 NLP evaluation

NLP suggests checking the congruence and ecology for the goal/outcome, using Cartesian Logic as shown in Figure 3.5. We can apply to quality management programme.

Converse	*Theorem*
~AB	**AB**
Example	Example
What would not happen if you did ___?	What would happen if you did ___?
Non-Mirror Image Reverse	*Inverse*
~A~B	**A~B**
Example	Example
What would not happen if you did not ___?	What would happen if you did not ___?

Figure 3.5 Cartesian coordinate

What would happen if we implement QMS? This clearly looks at the gains. Quality Management will deliver the following benefits:

- Consistency in product/service
- Market share improvement
- Defect reduction
- Productivity improvement—cycle time reduction
- Improved information flow
- Improved teamwork

What would not happen if we implement QMS? This looks at the loss of current practices or current benefits.

- Freedom to use your own way of doing work
- Work done during the audits

What would happen if we didn't implement QMS? This will look at the cost of continuing with current status or having status quo.

- Loss of competitive edge because of not doing quality improvement
- Continued high cost due to poor quality

What would not happen if we didn't implement QMS (did not achieve the outcome)? This is a difficult question. Logically, you may think of not making gains. It is best to answer the question intuitively rather than logically.

- Business will not happen as new innovation with improved quality can replace existing product/service

3.13 In Summary

Several quality models and frameworks have been developed over the last thirty years. Some are generic and some are industry specific. Organisations have several choices. These models and frameworks are supported by business processes. Organisations need to analyse the models and framework with careful mapping of business processes to the model or framework.

Organisations should consider different aspects as well as different business scenario to evaluate the model. NLP's Cartesian coordinates are useful in evaluation.

4

Continual Improvement

Quality management programme is a transformation programme. Many consultants will suggest a project management approach. Project will have end date (probably after achieving the goal of certification or award); project team will get dissolved after that date, and quality drive may run out of steam. Continual improvement programme is an ongoing and a growing programme. Stephen Convey mentioned in the seventh habit (sharpen the saw) the upward spiral with learn, commit, and do—learn, commit, and do . . . this continues. Continual improvement programme is similar. It follows cycles and grows. We should not fit continual improvement programme into project (with end date). We should fit projects into continual improvement cycle.

This chapter will discuss quality management approach and NLP approach.

4.1 P-D-C-A Cycle

Deming promoted P-D-C-A cycle. This is the simple concept for continual improvements. This concept is implemented in ISO 9001 and is also a part of service improvement in ISO 20000. ITIL also gives a separate module continual service improvement. Figure 4.1 shows the P-D-C-A cycle.

Plan

This step sets the objectives to be achieved. The objectives can be governed by vision, mission, long-term plans, and governance requirements. This step focuses on changes to be implemented for the process or product or services and determines how to measure effectiveness of changes. The objectives can be expressed in SMART manner (Specific, Measurable, Attainable, Realistic, and Timely)

Do

This step requires implementing the Change on smaller scale or there will be pilot implementation. Data is gathered. Based on data, charts are prepared and analysed.

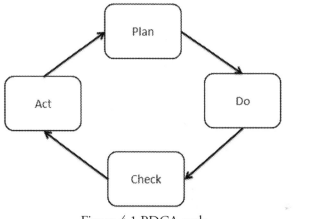

Figure 4.1 PDCA cycle

Check

This step measures the effect of the change. Review is conducted to compare the actual results for expected results (i.e., benefits). This provides the feedback on implementation and inputs for corrective or preventive action.

Act

If change is successful, accept the change as a permanent modification to the process. If change is not successful, the implementation can be with corrective action or these will be the inputs for the next cycle starting with plan again.

Over the time period, PDCA will bring a new baseline for the quality of product or service. Figure 4.2 shows it diagrammatically. Next cycle starts with plan for further quality improvement.

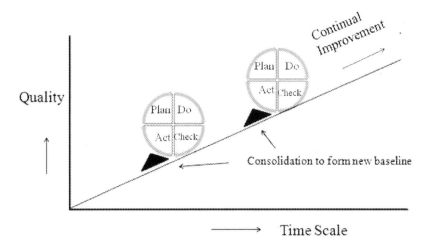

Figure 4.2 PDCA and continual improvement

4.2 Cycle of Generative Success

Cycle of Generative Success is a cycle or spiral (in case of three dimensions) that can provide success in your endeavours. Nothing succeeds like success. Two-dimensional cycle of generative success is shown in Figure 4.3.

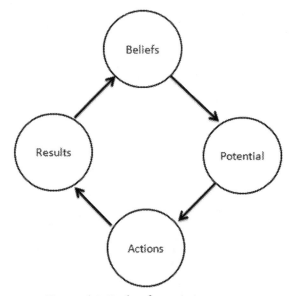

Figure 4.3 Cycle of generative success

Let us consider sports situations with two cricket batsmen.

Belief

Beliefs and values are the foundation for the success. (more discussion on belief and values is in Chapter 5) Let us consider two cricket batsmen. Cricket batsman A is 5' 6" in height and has a lean body. Another batsman B is 6' in height and has an athletic personality. If A believes that he is a good batsman and has the ability to tackle any bowler, he will have the confidence. If B believes that he is not a good batsman, he will show lack of confidence. Though B may be physically strong, he will not be a good batsman as compared to A.

Potential (Capability)

Potential is a personal power to succeed. As per NLP, everyone has the potential. Belief will influence the tapping of potential. Batsman A will build capabilities by tapping potential. He will develop skills to play against different kind of bowlers. Batsman B will look at limitation and explore the excuses for those limitations. Batsman A will be in better conditioning of body and mind.

Action (Behaviour)

Actions are the ones that will produce the results. Execution will not happen without the potential. Batsman A will display through his behaviour. He will watch other great batsmen. He will walk to the crease with confidence. His feet will move with assurance that he is going to play the best shot. In case of Batsman B, little potential will have little action. His confidence will be low and he will face ball with fear.

Results

When action is taken with full potential, the results will be good and meet the expectations. Good results will reinforce the belief. In the case of Batsman A, he will make runs and will get half-century or century. This result will boost his belief that he is a good batsman. Batsman B gets out with low score.

In short, Batsman A is on upward or ascending cycle with improving his performance. Batsman B is on downward or descending cycle. Batsman B would like to work on his results. Changing results are possible when he starts working on his belief that will tap higher potential. He should model behaviour of Batsman A. He can also produce results like Batsman A.

P- Plan D - Do C - Check A - Act   B - Belief P - Potential A - Action R - Result

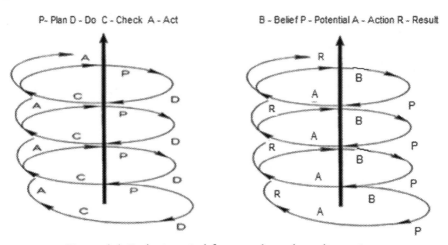

Figure 4.4 Cycles in spiral form to show three dimensions

In three dimensional view, PDCA cycle and generative success cycle become upward spiral. Figure 4.4 shows the same. We can combine both cycles and apply to business. Belief and behaviour of people working on improvements can impact the success of improvements.

Belief (Conceptual planning)

When an organisation develops new products or sets stretched goals, it may look impossible for others. However, the organisation has to have a belief that they will succeed in the achievement of goals. Some of the examples of product/process development are as follows:

- In the '70s, Sony Senior Executive was at the airport in the United States. He saw an Afro-American having a big cassette player. He was enjoying the music, but it was causing annoyance for others. Sony Senior executive believed there can be a device which will allow a person to listen without disturbing others. Sony believed the organisation's technical expertise on miniaturising the product. The technical team of Sony designed and marketed the product called 'Walkman' successfully.

- In the late nineteenth century, offices had a complex machine called typewriter. People used two-fingered typing called 'hunt and peck'. Frank McGurrin believed that typing without looking at the keys is faster. People commented, 'That's silly. Who could possibly do that?' McGurrin developed and taught touch typing. However, later, people realised touch typing is the effective way of using typewriter.

Organisation needs to believe in a new concept. Wright brothers believed in flying machine, hence they could built it. For quality improvement, organisation and the people working on improvement should have strong belief.

Build capability and plan

Organisation can provide trainings, and employees can develop skills to build capability of the organisation. Organisation can tap the potential of employees. It is interesting to question whether an organisation utilises the potential of the employee to the fullest.

The resource for capability is the brains of the employees. Brain is divided into two: left brain and right brain. Left brain is related to logical, sequential, rational, analytical, and objective thinking, whereas right brain is related to random, intuitive, holistic, synthesising, and subjective thinking.

If we wish to utilise our full potential, we need to use the left as well as the right brain. NLP exercises are useful for conditioning the right-brain abilities.

Plan means giving concrete steps to the concept or belief. We will build a strategy for execution.

Do and behave

This step will implement the plan or execute strategy. This is a pilot implementation or working on prototype. It is an understanding of the plan and use of capabilities to perform the activities.

Behaviour is related to having the resourceful states of mind. These can be confidence, creativity, or any other positive states. Behaviour reflects the beliefs.

Check

This step will validate the results achieved. As per NLP presupposition, there is no failure, only feedback. Continual improvement also means continual learning. When results are not satisfactory, there will be learning. One powerful example is Thomas Alva Edison inventing a light bulb. For the failure, his comment was 'he knows 1,000 ways that light bulb will not function'.

Act

This step will look at changes required to the plan or new strategy for implementation. As per NLP presupposition, if what you are doing is not working, do something else.

Successful results will reinforce the beliefs and initiate implementation across the organisation.

4.3 Limiting Belief

Limiting belief can pose constraint in improvement. Here is Birbal's story

Once, a scholar requested Emperor Akbar that he would like to test the intelligence of his courtiers. Akbar permitted him. The courtiers gathered in the palace at the agreed hour. The scholar kept a covered pot before them and asked them to tell what the pot contained. There was complete silence as there was no clue. Then Birbal stepped forwards and removed the cover. He said, 'It is empty.'

The annoyed scholar said, 'But you opened it.'

Birbal replied, 'You did not say we could not open it.'

The scholar could not argue. He bowed to the emperor and left the court.

4.4 Modified PDCA/Continual Improvement

Most of the quality management frameworks have incorporated PDCA in them. ISO 9001 has clause 8.5.1 to address the continual improvement. ITIL has a separate ongoing phase 'Continual Service Improvement'. It is across other four ITIL phases—Service strategy, Service design, Service transition, and Service operation. COBIT 5 has a life cycle approach, and continual improvement life cycle is at the core of three interrelated components. COBIT 5 has integrated continual improvement with two components—programme management and change management.

Table 4.1 shows the extended or modified PDCA in ITIL and COBIT. For more details, we can refer to ITIL books and COBIT document.

ITIL	COBIT
• Identify strategy for improvement	• Recognise need to act
	• Assess current state
• Define what you will measure	• Define target state
• Gather the data	• Build improvements
• Process data	• Implement improvement
• Analyse information and data	• Operate and measure
• Present and use information	• Monitor and evaluate
• Implement improvement	

Table 4.1 Steps in continual improvement in ITIL and COBIT

4.5 Change House

Swedish psychologist Claes Janssen developed a concept 'Four Rooms of Change'. Robbie Steinhouse modified and developed 'Change House' (shown in Figure 4.5).

For an individual, 'Change House' concept is as follows:

Our happy time is the room of contentment. We are in a comfort zone and enjoy the state. Occasionally, we experience the ecstasy in sun deck.

Life is not always smooth. Certain events happen, and our bad time starts. We get rejection for our plans or for our wish. We experience denials. This is the room of denial. Sometimes, things go from bad to worse. As the situation worsens, we are in a room of despair.

However, we look for the silver lining. We are not sure about the future. We are in a state of confusion. We are in a room of confusion. When we take an incorrect decision, it is the entry to the wrong door. We will be back in the room of confusion.

Soon, we analyse the situation, utilise all learning, and generate ideas. Finally, we come up with renewal strategy. This is the room of renewal.

With successful implementation of the strategy, we are back in the room of containment.

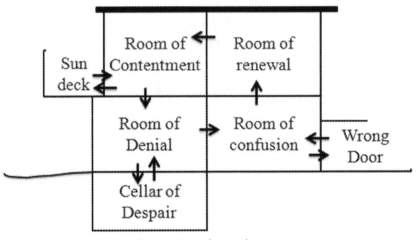

Figure 4.5 Change house

Change house can be applied to the business. In a room of contentment, an organisation has a steady business with growth at satisfactory level. Other indicators like market share, profitability, share price, employee satisfaction, customer satisfaction, and operational efficiencies show good results. Quality programmes' focus will be monitoring risk to the business and developing products or services for future. With booming economy, the organisation's performance can be excellent (sun deck).

Businesses always have threats as well as opportunities. Michael Porter provided five forces model, which are as follows:

- Competitive rivalry within industry
- Threat of new entrant
- Threat of substitute product
- Bargaining power of customer
- Bargaining power of supplier

The other example of threats can be labour unrest or financial blunders. In the room of denial, organisation will be making losses, loss of market share, or drop in share price (market capitalisation). When the organisation is insolvent, it is the cellar of despair. In the case of room of denial, quality programme will focus on problem solving.

Organisation will be in a confused state as it will have challenges on every front—financial distress, operational inefficiencies, and loss of market. This is the room of confusion. Organisation will revisit learning and analyse the situation. Organisation will look for financial restructuring, optimisation of operations, and marketing strategies. With the renewal strategy, the organisation moves into the room of renewal. Quality programme will look into improvements in all aspects.

When renewal strategy delivers the results, organisation is back in the room of contentment.

If we consider 'Change house' concept, quality programme focuses on how to move to the room of contentment and remain in the room of containment. It is similar to the aim of continual improvements.

4.6 Product Life Cycle and Value Cycle

Change house has room of contentment and room of despair. We can remain in the house of contentment when a customer sees the value in our products. If customers feel they are not getting worth of the cost they are paying, the business organisation will be out of business and will be in a room of despair. We need to understand the position of the product in the market and value for the customer. Boston Consultancy Group (BCG) provides the growth-share matrix to look at product status. It is shown in figure 4.6

Growth rate	High	Star	Question mark
	Low	Cash Cow	Dog
		High	Low
		Market Share	

Figure 4.6 BCG growth share matrix

Organisation develops several products (and/or services). These are in quadrant 'question mark'. The organisation picks up a few products which can move to the quadrant 'Star'. Star products are high growth and high market share. Remaining products (in question mark) will be divested. Organisation will invest more in Star products. Soon product will mature and the growth rate will drop. Product moves to quadrant 'Cash Cow'. The high market share continues and provides good revenue. Organisation will invest less in Cash Cow products. Later, demand for product declines. The market share is low and growth is low. Product is quadrant 'dog'. Product will be discontinued.

The successful product from quadrant 'Star' and 'Cash Cow' will keep an organisation in the room of containment. The room of confusion is quadrant 'Question Mark'. The room of despair is quadrant 'Dog'. Success sequence or cycle is Question Mark → Star → Cow → Question Mark. Unsuccessful sequence will end up with quadrant 'Dog'.

John Guaspari has given a model on how a customer values a product. When products are introduced (quadrant 'question mark'), it is availability of product. Quality programme will be more focused on quality of design and creativity to develop a new product. The value proposition is product leadership. There will be few players in the market. For example, cell phones or mobile phones were made available. This is a star product stage.

At the next stage, more organisations enter into the market where reliability of product plays an important role. In the case of cell phone, customers expect less maintenance that is, high reliability. Process quality plays an important role in providing consistent and reliable product/services. Organisations' quality programmes will focus on process quality improvement. This stage is cash cow. The value proposition is operational excellence.

To remain in market, the next phase is to have suitability. In the case of cell phone, its weight, size, and thickness, screen, and additional functions will give value to the customers. More products will provide a variety of suitable features. The value proposition is through customer intimacy.

Next phase will be flexibility. Customer sees flexibility in using product. The value proposition continues with customer intimacy and deeper understanding of customers' needs and wants. In the case of cell phone, customers started using as FM radio and MP3 player. Thus, there is flexibility in the usage of cell phone. After phase 4, it is time to introduce or make available new product with mobile computing (for example, maybe tablet pc). The phases and important quality attributes are shown in Figure 4.7.

Phase 1	Phase 2	Phase 3	Phase 4
			Flexibility
		Suitability	Suitability
	Reliability	Reliability	Reliability
Availability	Availability	Availability	Availability
Phase 1	Phase 2	Phase 3	Phase 4

Figure 4.7 Product life cycle and quality focus

Quality programme needs to support the quality requirement as per the required stage of the product life cycle.

4.7 Benchmarking

Benchmarking has been practiced as a part of continual improvement. The current practice or process is compared with the best practices. In case of metrics benchmarking, the performance indicators are compared. It is useful to identify the performance gap. In case of process benchmarking, process is compared and examined to improve. Benchmarking within organisation is considered as internal benchmarking. Benchmarking with other organisation is considered as external benchmarking.

Xerox, the leading copier company, used benchmarking extensively and successfully under the programme, 'Leadership through Quality'. The benchmarking process at Xerox has ten steps in four phases. These are as follows:

- Phase 1—Planning

    o Step 1: Identify what to benchmark
    o Step 2: Identify comparative companies
    o Step 3: Determine the data collection method and collect data

- Phase 2—Analysis

    o Step 4: Determine current performance gap
    o Step 5: Project future performance levels

- Phase 3—Integration

  o Step 6: Communicate benchmark findings and gain acceptance
  o Step 7: Establish functional goals

- Phase 4—Action

  o Step 8: Develop action plan
  o Step 9: Implement specific actions and monitor progress
  o Step 10: Recalibrate benchmarks

4.8 Modelling (NLP Concept)

We have seen Quality Guru in Chapter 3. As a quality professional, we would like to be like them. We would like to benchmark them. Benchmarking process may not help in personal benchmarking. However, NLP has a solution. NLP gives a tool called 'Modelling' to adopt all required qualities. Modelling is behavioural modelling to identify unconscious competence of an expert. The competence can be classified as behavioural, cognitive, and linguistic with further classification as simple and complex.

The generic steps are—

- Identify an expert to model the skills
- Find his/her values, beliefs, and other filters like meta programme (refer to Appendix A: NLP Communication Model)
- Find his/her strategies
- Find his/her motivation
- Perform contrast analysis—This is to find the essential elements and dropping idiosyncrasy.
- Perform sensitivity analysis—Test the essential elements to confirm that the desired change is observed
- Derive strategy used—Find what they do in their head when experts work or use their skills.
- Install strategies and work like an expert.
- Design the training programme to train people on the skill.

We can use NLP modelling to replicate the best performer or combine NLP modelling with benchmarking. Combined process will ensure that the functional goals will be achieved. Figure 4.8 shows the relationship among three benchmarking. Steps 8 and 9 (Section 4.6) can include NLP modelling.

Metric benchmarking can identify the area for improvements or processes for improvement. This looks at the performance indicator and shows the gap. This is at the highest level.

Process benchmarking examines the procedure, and gaps in process steps are identified for improvements. At high level, it is good to look at the purpose of the process. For example, same process at charity hospitals and at commercial hospitals will differ. This is at the middle level with more information.

Behavioural benchmarking is NLP modelling. This is very detailed information on behaviour. This will look at—

- Non-verbal communication
- Interaction among different roles
- Relationship management by different role takers

Figure 4.8 Benchmarking integrated with behavioural study

Benchmarking can be illustrated with an example. Let us consider incident management process of IT department. IT department is owner of this process and user departments use it when they have some issue with IT system. This process is part of ITIL under phase service operations and also is a part of COBIT under 'deliver, service and support'. Let us define it in brief (Reference: COBIT 5 and ITIL v3)

- Purpose: To provide timely and effective response and resolution to all types of incidents. To achieve increased productivity and minimise disruption through a quick resolution of incidents.
- Metrics: Performance indicators are

  o Number of incident affecting availability of IT system for critical business process
  o Mean time to resolve incident
  o Percentage of incidents resolved within Service Level Agreement (SLA)
  o User satisfaction on incident management

- Process: RACI chart for Incident Management process (R—Responsibility, A—Accountable, C—Consult and I—Inform) is given in Table 4.2.

Activity	Service Desk	IT Analyst	Incident Manager	User
Record, classify and prioritise an incident	R	A		C
Investigate, diagnose and allocate incident	R	A		
Resolve and recover from incident.		R	A	
Close incident		R		C
Track status and produce reports			R	

Table 4.2 RACI for incident management process

There are two IT departments supporting the business A and B. Both IT departments decide to assess their incident management process and find the opportunities.

First, both IT departments looked at metrics captured for the incident management process. As shown in Table 4.3, last quarter's data was—

Metric	IT Department A	IT Department B
Number of Incident affecting critical processes	4	5
Mean time to resolve incident	2 Hrs	2.2 Hrs
Percentage of incidents resolved within SLA	95%	93%
User satisfaction on incident management	75	80

Table 4.3Incident metrics

Department B is interested to know faster resolution by Department A. Department A is interested to know higher user satisfaction achieved by the Department B.

At second level, both departments looked at incident management process.

Both departments looked at process steps. Incident classification and prioritisation definition were checked, and computation of metrics were confirmed. In addition, first-time resolution by service desk using knowledge database and escalation of unresolved incidents to analyst is of interest to the users. More detailed analysis of process steps will provide improvement opportunities and also the metrics to measure and compare.

At the third level, both departments looked at the behaviour aspects. These include—

- Interacting with others: Service desk needs to interact with users to record an incident. Service desk needs to record incident properly so that the analyst understands it to resolve it. Analysts need to interact with users upon resolution and to close the incident.
- Managing relationship: The service desk person and IT analyst need to have flexibility to handle different types of users—irate, indecisive, insistent, friendly, or cooperative.
- Non-verbal communication: As per NLP, our body and mind are connected. The mental states like confidence and creativity can be

regained through body posture. Non-verbal communication also plays an important role in creating rapport.

The higher user satisfaction for department B could be achieved through having rapport during interaction and building relationship.

4.9 Connecting Continual Improvement to Certifications and Compliance

Organisations have long-term plans. Some organisations look forwards to certifications like ISO 9000 or ISO 20000, some organisations wish to comply with COBIT, and some organisations wish to win Quality Award. All these plans need to be connected with continual improvement.

We can divide the plan in smaller chunks and make the plan into incremental implementation and integration plan (IIIP).

As discussed in Chapter 1, section of employees will be motivated by certification or compliance. Rest of them need other motivational strategies. Hence, we need to take bigger picture and include their needs related to quality. The annual (or as the organisation defines a period) quality improvement plan is prepared. This plan will include the increment from incremental implementation and integration plan (IIIP).

Teams (or departments) execute the annual quality improvement plan. Incremental implementation and integration plan (IIIP) integrates and confirms full compliance and readiness for certification.

4.10 Be Alert and Keep Momentum

Business needs to be vigilant about the business environment and keep momentum through continual improvement. The following story of frogs can illustrate this point.

The story is about a scientist experimenting with frogs. The scientist took two frogs of the same size. He had two pots also of the same size. The first pot had hot water close to boiling point and it was not on flame to heat further. The second pot had lukewarm water and was on flame to heat it further slowly to boiling point in an hour.

The scientist threw the first frog into the first pot. The frog sensed the heat and jumped out of the hot water with minor burns.

The scientist threw the second frog into the second pot. The frog enjoyed the warmth; it could not realise the increase in temperature and finally died.

Then the scientist took two more frogs of the same size. They were in water. The first frog was active, swimming, and jumping, but the second frog was lethargic. The scientist then poured milk in two pots. Both were moved to the pots with milk.

The first frog continued to swim energetically in the milk. The second frog made efforts sluggishly.

In the case of the first frog, cream was formed soon in the milk. The frog jumped on the cream and came out of the pot successfully.

In the case of the second frog, there was a struggle for survival.

4.11 In Summary

Businesses are dynamic and continuously evolving. To match this, a business organisation needs continual improvement programme. Traditional quality management provides P-D-C-A and benchmarking. These can be altered with NLP concepts, and we added important elements—beliefs and behaviour.

Modelling can complement the benchmarking exercise, and the success of benchmarking gets the assurance.

The business also needs to look at product life cycle. Quality programme should be agile to reflect the needs of product life cycle and status of business expressed with change house concept.

5

Quality Management System

Quality Management System (QMS), as per ISO 9000 definition, is management system to direct and control organisation with respect to quality. Good business leaders do not differentiate between quality and business. They understand that quality is embedded in every aspect of business. Quality Management System becomes business management system.

This chapter will discuss QMS structure, QMS with reference to the neurological levels. QMS with reference to wheel of life, QMS, and 3S (system, strategy, and synergy) and QMS based on value chain.

When we rotate kaleidoscope, it shows the same pieces with different structure and we could see different perspective. We will use kaleidoscope approach to QMS.

5.1 QMS Structure

Typical QMS structure will suggest three or four-tier documents. Quality Manual is a top-level document. It will state the quality policy and quality objectives. The next level is procedures. This may be divided into two: procedures across organisation and procedure at department level. The lowest level is forms and templates. This level will form records of the system. This QMS structure is shown in Figure 5.1.

If an organisation follows ISO 9001 standards, quality manual is prepared, and it will define the quality policy and quality objectives. Quality policy should be appropriate to the purpose of the organisation and quality objectives are measurable and aligned to the quality policy.

It is a challenge to ensure that QMS is aligned with the business.

Consultant may use his or her templates, and 'copy and paste' formula will lead to improper alignment. QMS can be viewed as a part of business, using neurological levels.

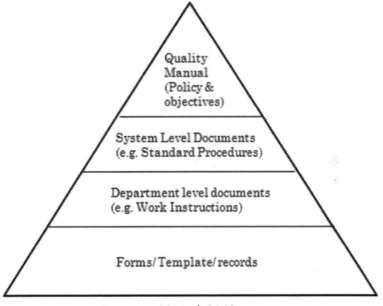

Figure 5.1 Typical QMS structure

5.2 Neurological Levels

Robert Dilts developed neurological levels based on concept by anthropologist Gregory Bateson. Figure 5.2 shows the neurological levels. This can be applied to an organisation and will be useful understand the link among the various levels. Then we can also place QMS elements (policy, objectives, processes and so on) at appropriate levels. This will help the integration of QMS with the business.

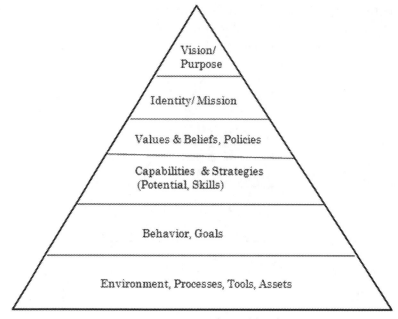

Figure 5.2 Neurological levels

An important aspect of the neurological level is impact. If a change is made at a certain level, all levels below that level are impacted. For example, employee's performance is not satisfactory, and manager advocates transferring that employee to another department. His performance in new department is also dissatisfactory. The change at environment level (that is level six) could not solve the problem. If we look at the employee's performance issue with neurological levels, we can check the employee's capabilities (that is level four) with reference to the performance. If we provide training to develop the capabilities, the performance will improve. There can be issue at belief level (that is level three). His negative or limiting belief is resulting in underutilisation of capabilities and impacting the performance. Change in belief will improve the performance of the employee.

The QMS should not be seen in isolation and should be grouped with appropriate neurological levels. If QMS is considered at environment level (which is the lowest), it will not have impact on behaviour level and will not have much significance to the higher levels.

Neurological levels will also look at alignment among different levels. Any misalignment will have impact on performance of the organisation.

Let us explore each level.

1. Purpose/Vision: This is the most important thing an organisation wants to do. It is a conceptual and purposeful foresight. An organisation can look ten or twenty years ahead and develop the vision. It provides your connection to a larger system—community, country, and world. This will provide the organisation's highest intention to serve its customer (or stakeholders).

    We can look at vision statement of the organisations from their website. For example, let us look at vision of commercial conglomerate ITC (reference www.itcportal.com) and non-profit organisation Toastmasters International.

    Vision of ITC is 'Sustain ITC's position as one of India's most valuable corporations through world class performance, creating growing value for the Indian economy and the Company's stakeholders'

    Vision of Toastmasters (Reference—Pat Johnson International President 'Viewpoint: Living the Vision') is 'Toastmasters International [you and I] empowers people to achieve their full potential and realise their dreams. Through our member clubs, people throughout the world can improve their communication and leadership skills, and find the courage to change'.

    From a quality perspective, ITC is looking at world-class performance, value growth, and addresses all stakeholders; Toastmasters is looking at achieving full potential and realisation of the dream.

2. Identity/Mission: This is an internally focused statement, setting direction and governance. Mission shows how vision will be achieved. This answers the question who are you (as an organisation). Hence, mission statement can include the products and services provided and overall strategy for long-term success.

    We can refer to ITC and Toastmasters for Mission.

    ITC's mission is 'to enhance the wealth generating capability of the enterprise in a globalising environment, delivering superior and sustainable stakeholder value'.

    Toastmasters' mission is 'to provide a mutually supportive and positive learning environment in which every individual member has the opportunity to develop oral communication and leadership skills, which, in turn, foster self-confidence and personal growth'.

From a quality perspective, ITC indicates the capability to achieve the vision; Toastmasters indicates what it provides to achieve its vision.

3. Values, Beliefs, and Policies: These are factors that are important to the organisation for working situations. These are like compass that guides the decisions and makes out what is right and what is wrong. Organisations need to nurture the desired values to support the mission. Policies are statements that give the management intention. Policies give guidance on how to put values into practice.

    We can refer to ITC and Toastmasters for their values.

    ITC's values (reference www.itcportal.com) are trusteeship, customer focus, respect for people, excellence, innovation, and nation orientation. Toastmasters' values are integrity, respect, service, and excellence.

    From a quality perspective, values like excellence, innovation, customer focus, and so on, directly depict quality. Values like service, respect, integrity, and so on, have great impact on quality.

    Values are further discussed in Sections 5.4 and 5.5.

4. Capability and strategies: Capabilities are skills, competencies, and knowledge of an organisation. Strategies are the long-term plans, medium-term plans, and short-term plans.

    An organisation gets the competitive advantage through capabilities and strategies. Organisations can see the current and future business requirement and build ability and capacity through training and developing the systems.

    ITC (reference www.itcportal.com) has very diversified business— FMCG (Fast Moving Consumer Goods): Hotels, Packaging, Information Technology, Agriculture-based business and so on. The sustainability achieved is through strategies adopted and capabilities built.

    Toastmasters International has focused on education in leadership and communication through experiential learning in toastmasters club. In 2013, Toastmasters International has 292,000 members in 14,350 clubs in 122 countries who are using the structured programme. The capability reflects through systematic functioning of club and providing structured educational programme.

From a quality perspective, quality of service and products will depend on capabilities of the organisation.

5. Behaviour: This is the behaviour of people in the organisation. This is the experience people get in the organisation. The behaviour has impact of all above levels. This gives reason for people to stay with the organisation.

   In case of ITC (reference www.itcportal.com), employees appreciate the flexibility, support, and motivation from superior, emphasis on excellence, training, learning and so on.

   In the case of toastmasters, members and guests in the club meetings experience the opportunities for speaking, systematic feedback, and culture of learning from each other.

   From a quality perspective, people will be able to perform the quality work when they are comfortable at the workplace.

6. Environment: These are the process or procedures defining where, when, and who will perform activity. The role and responsibilities are clearly defined. There is a certainty and no ad-hoc approach to the work.

   In case of ITC (reference www.itcportal.com), Quality Management System is built on national and international standards and also based on the best practices.

   In the case of toastmasters, club meeting roles, club officers' role, and district officers' role and responsibilities are well defined and set the expectation at right level.

   From a quality perspective, processes and system provide the base for the quality product and services.

Some organisation may put mission over vision because missionary zeal impacts the organisation more than the visionaries' appetite. However, considering external focus of vision statement and internal focus of mission statement, we will consider vision is supported by mission. Quality Management System (QMS) should be structured based on neurological levels.

5.3 Crafting Vision and Mission

Neurological levels 1 and 2 are Vision and Mission of the organisation. For crafting the vision, the following questions are useful:

- What does the organisation do well (quality work—product or services)?
- What is the most important thing the organisation wants to do (achievement that signifies quality)?
- What makes the organisation unique or special (Innovative as a part of quality)?
- What make the teams feel good about the organisation? (affiliation or people quality)
- What is the organisation plan for future five/ten/twenty years?
- What are the organisation's aspiration and inspiration?

Vision statement should be clear, simple, and generic.

For crafting the mission, the following questions are useful:

- What are the primary products and services of the organisation? (link to organisation's capability)
- What is the distinctive competitive advantage for the organisation? (link to organisation's capability and strategy)
- What is the overall strategy for long-term success? (link to organisation's strategy)
- What are the organisation values and beliefs? (link to values and belief)
- How will the mission portray the broader goal of the organisation? (link to vision)
- How will the mission cause those involved with the organisation to act positively?
- How will the mission implement a broad tone and attitude that guides the organisation?

Mission statements will be short with three to five sentences—general, flexible, strategic, and motivating in nature.

An organisation can conduct a brainstorming session, involving different people. Vision and mission are applicable to the whole organisation. Departments or teams should look at their contribution for achieving the vision and ensure adherence to the values.

If departments or teams have their own vision and mission, then organisation will suffer lack of teamwork and lack of synergy, and the organisation will not be effective or successful.

5.4 Belief, Values, Attitude, and Behaviour

It is important to understand the relationship among beliefs, values, attitude, and behaviour. We can use analogy of water plant. If we visit the countryside, we can see water lily or lotus plants. We can see a flowers and leaves. The rest of the plant is invisible as it is under water. In the case of people, we can see their behaviour. Their beliefs, values, and attitude are underneath.

Beliefs are like roots of water plants and are clustered around values (values are like stem). Beliefs are convictions or acceptances that certain things are true or real. If a person has beliefs like honesty is the best policy, an honest person has integrity, and that an honest person is reliable person, his value is honesty, and there are beliefs around the value.

Attitudes are collection of values and belief systems around a certain subject. Thus, attitude is at a higher level of abstraction. Attitude towards quality influences the way work is done and the success of the quality programme.

A person or manager with a positive attitude towards quality considers having quality records as part of accountability. The behaviour is proper housekeeping of records. The manager (person) sees a quality audit as an opportunity for feedback or improvement.

A person or manager with negative attitude towards quality considers having quality records as bureaucracy. The behaviour is unorganised quality records. The manager (person) sees a quality audit as an unnecessary evil to face as he or she needs work around for organising the quality records.

5.5 Value and Values

We need to have a good understanding of the term 'value' and 'values'.

In Chapter 4, we discussed the value of a product. This value is in the commercial sense. This value is the ratio of 'what the customer GOT' to 'what it COST to the customer'. To extend this term to the organisation, organisations will look at market capitalisation (in case of an organisation listed at stock exchange) or assets and goodwill (in case of other business). For successful quality programme, we need to have a good understanding of value creation. In case of neurological levels, value creation needs to be addressed in levels 4, 5, and 6.

In Chapter 5, we discussed values of a person or an organisation. This value is linked to morality or ethics. This operates at neurological level 3 and will impact all levels below (levels 4, 5, and 6). For successful quality programme, values play an influential role. Quality leadership nurtures values for quality.

TV Rao described HRD values in his book *Managers Who Make a Difference*. We can look at HRD values (acronym OCTAPACE) and their influence on quality.

- Openness: Employees, irrespective of their position, should have freedom to express their ideas and opinion. Openness is necessary for quality initiatives like staff suggestion scheme and also for brainstorming sessions for product design or problem solving.
- Collaboration: This is employees' readiness to seek help from others and to provide help to others. This is essential for high performance of teams and implement quality concept 'internal customer'.
- Trust and trustworthiness: This is to accept thing at face value. As an organisation develops processes and prefers quality assurance over quality control, trust on system, process, and people is necessary for successful transition. Lack of trust results in costly quality control activities, and the organisation cannot move from quality control to quality assurance.
- Authenticity: This is about speaking truth and not hiding the fact. This is important for quality as executives as well as management not ready to face bad news. This leads to quality reporting with some window dressing. As Deming suggest, we need to drive out fear so that reliable reporting happens.
- Pro-action: This means taking initiative, generating more options, and choosing the best option. The quality concept 'preventive actions' will happen when people are proactive and not reactive.
- Autonomy: This is the freedom of discretion in the job. This encourages to suggest improvements in the processes and

to develop the best practices for the processes. For quality improvements, autonomy is required.

- Confrontation: This is to face the issue squarely and taking up challenges. If we hide the issues, they can turn into bigger problems. For quality management, early detection is important, and this, in turn, will help early resolution.
- Experimentation: This is to work on innovation. Innovation is possible when there is experimentation. Even failed experiments will increase the knowledge.

There may be a question as to how many values we should have as we can have a long list of values for the organisation. In reality, values are in hierarchical form and thus select four or five top values. Other supporting values will be covered by the top values. For example, trust will be built when there is authenticity, and authenticity is possible when there is openness. Thus, we can select trust as the highest value.

We need to analyse our values that support vision and mission (higher neurological levels) and influence our strategies, behaviour, decisions, and system functioning. Hence, it is necessary to find true values we display through our behaviour or decisions. If the organisation states values that are good to have, then there will be misalignment, and the organisation will face challenges. For example, Enron had four values—Respect, Integrity, Communication, and Excellence. However, the behaviour was displaying the opposite side of those values.

If employees' values differ from the organisation's values, they will feel uncomfortable and may leave the organisation soon.

The important point is elicitation of values of leader(s) and how they want to lead the organisation. NLP master practitioner can help the elicitation of values. For setting up QMS, values are to be taken care in the following way:

- Elicit the values of leader(s). Resolve conflicting values.
- Use hierarchy of values to get top four or five values. Understand the link with quality.
- Check the alignment with mission and vision.
- Communicate values, and explain how they should be practiced and walk the talk (if behaviour is not aligned with values like respect, people will perceive the values like arrogance exhibited by the behaviour).

- Bring out personal and organisational stories about values.
- Apply zero-tolerance for violating the values.
- Review values along with vision and mission at defined intervals (as per long-term plan or every three years).

5.6 Leadership and Quality

Neurological levels also provide the leadership style to adopt. Quality programme needs transformational leadership. Transformational leadership operates at higher levels.

- Charismatic leadership: The leader has vision and mission. He (or she) provides the common purpose for the organisation. There is idealised influence.
- Individualised leadership: The leader acts as a coach or mentor. The leader develops talents by giving individual attention.
- Inspirational leadership: The leader instils the values and inspires to do the best.
- Intellectual stimulation: The leader strengthens the beliefs and gives challenging ideas.
- Management by objectives: The leader understands the potential, skills, and capabilities. The leader will motivate to achieve higher capabilities by setting clear objectives.

Leadership using lower neurological levels is transactional leadership.

- Management using contingent rewards: The leader promises reward for good work (behaviour). The leader communicates the expected good work and gives special commendation for the efforts.
- Management by exception: The leader keeps track through monitoring the numbers. When numbers do not match as expected, the leader intervenes and asks for corrective action.

5.7 Wheel of Life

As an individual, if we wish to have balance in different aspects of life, we can use the wheel of life. When we set a goal in one area, we can assess any conflict with other areas and achieve a balanced life. If we focus on work and money alone, we will spend more time and resources on the goals in this area. It may lead to poor health and poor relationship, and we may feel the fun missing. Figure 5.3 shows the wheel of life for an individual.

Figure 5.3 Wheel of life—individual

Let us map this wheel of life to the organisation. It is shown in Figure 5.4. Some NLP trainings may consider a subset—money, career, health, family, and so on, by picking up five or six aspects of life. The wheel in Figure 5.4 is comprehensive. These cover a wide range of stakeholders—investors/shareholders, employees, regulators, customers, suppliers, society and so on. If there are more stakeholders and the organisation has a goal related those stakeholders, then add component to the wheel of life.

The quality management system (or business management system) should look at all the components of the wheel. The goals set in each component of the wheel should be balanced with the other components of the wheel. Each component is a big subject in its own right, and a subject matter expert will contribute to QMS. The brief introduction is as follows:

1. Financial results: These are important for a profit-making organisation to give a good return on investment to the shareholders or investors. It is also important for a non-profit organisation because of effective utilisation funds for the cause.

2. Learning and development: In knowledge economy, this plays an important role in building intangible assets and market capitalisation. An organisation will look into technical skills and innovations as well as soft skills required for business.

3. Operational results: This is linked to business processes and their performance. The efficiency and effectiveness of processes indicate the operational results. The key performance indicators like cycle time, time to market shows the capabilities of the organisation.

4. Customer and supplier relationship: In value chain, we have the customer as a source of income and the supplier can be strategic alliance. The customer satisfaction, compliments, and complaints are important indicators for customer retention and future business. Supplier feeds the inputs to the business; the quality of inputs impacts the quality of products and services. Just-in-time programme is possible with collaborating with suppliers. Some organisations can include distributors in the value chain.

Figure 5.4 Wheel of life—organisation

5. Ethics and compliance: Organisations develop code of conduct to ensure business is run in an ethical manner. Some of the ethical issues arise due to conflict of interest or lack of integrity and honesty, intentional misuse of assets, or immoral behaviour. Organisations need to obey the laws of the country of its operation. In addition, there will be regulations from stock

exchange for the listed companies. The collapse of Enron in 2001 gave push for ethics and compliance. Sarbanes Oxley or SOX also strengthens the need for ethics and accountability.

6. Environment, safety, and health: Environment is important as our planet has limited resources and we will pay a heavy price for any damage to the environment. Several topics like waste management, waste water, air emission, hazardous materials management, energy conservation, water conservation, and so on, are under this umbrella. ISO 14000 standard is related to environment management system (EMS). Product and processes should be safe without any hazards and also without impact to the health.

7. Employee engagement and welfare: Employee engagement is the sense of belonging to the organisation among the employees. Engagement goes beyond satisfaction. Aon Hewitt's Adler suggests three questions to gauge the engagement of employees:

   • Say: Do they speak positively about the organisation?
   • Stay: Can employees envision staying with the same organisation long-term?
   • Strive: Are employees going above and beyond what they're required to do?

Employee welfare is about all those activities (like Insurance, Educational assistance) which provide some benefits other than remuneration.

8. Work environment: According to Confucius, 'Choose a job you love, and you will never have to work a day in your life'. If employees love their job, they will enjoy their work. Work environment should be enjoyable and free from stress. Work environment can have two major aspects: physical environment and human relational environment. Ergonomics will address the physical requirement of work environment like layout, noise-free comfortable temperature and so on. Human relation requires several soft skills like communication, teamwork, leadership and so on.

9. Corporate Social Responsibility: Many organisations understand their connection with the society and responsibility towards them. These organisations spend a good amount of money for social cause like education, health, and rural development. In

the case of a developing country, it is about nation building. ISO 26000 is related to Social Responsibility.

All these components interact, impact, and, sometimes, overlap each other. An organisation needs to have congruence (approximate similar importance) for these components. QMS will capture necessary information, processes related to these components.

Some organisations focus on one component: either financial results or customer first or employee first; this can result in imbalance. Many organisations have adopted a balanced scorecard and understood the importance of a balanced approach with four elements—finance, customer, internal processes, and learning and innovation. With wheel of life, we have further components to think about and more balanced approach towards running the business. Balanced Scorecard may have monthly reporting and review; however, monthly reporting for wheel of life can result in heavy overheads. It may be appropriate to review wheel of life once in six months.

5.8 System, Strategy, and Synergy (3S)

For achieving quality objectives or excellence, system alone will not be sufficient. It needs to be supported by strategy and synergy. It forms 3S. Figure 5.5 shows the neurological levels and their relation to strategy, synergy and system.

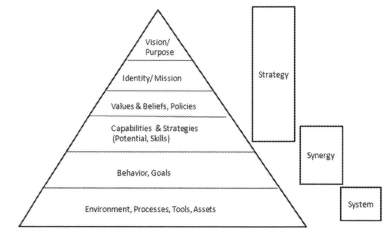

Figure 5.5 Neurological levels and 3S

Systems are the set of interrelated elements. These include the structures, processes, guidelines, tools, and techniques used by different functions of the organisation. The system also covers the utilisation of information technology and automation of processes. With reference to neurological levels, systems are at level 6 environment.

Synergy means a team producing more than the sum of the individual's contribution (production). This is about behaviour and collaboration of people. With reference to the neurological levels, it is at level 5 behaviour and also at capabilities (level 4) considering the soft skills.

Strategies are the plans that help to achieve the purpose and goals. Strategies are also necessary to optimum use of systems. Strategic thinking is required for defining vision and mission statements. With reference to neurological levels, strategies are at levels 1 to 4.

All three parameters can have eight combinations as shown in Figure 5.6.

		Synergy			
		Weak (-Sg)	Strong (+Sg)		
System	Strong (+Sm)	+Sm-Sg+St	+Sm+Sg+St	Strong (+St)	Strategy
		+Sm-Sg-St	+Sm+Sg-St	Weak (-St)	
	Weak (-Sm)	-Sm-Sg+St	-Sm+Sg+St	Strong (+St)	
		-Sm-Sg-St	-Sm+Sg-St	Weak (-St)	

Figure 5.6 System-Synergy-Strategy combinations

All combination can be seen with examples from airline industry. A customer goes through series of interactions or experiences, starts with enquiry and booking of tickets, then, on the day of travel, it is check-in, lounge wait, gate pass, in-flight, reaching destination, and baggage claim. Several systems, teams of people, and strategies of management are working to serve airline customers. Let us explore the combinations of System, Strategy, and Synergy (3S).

- –Sm–Sg–St: When systems, strategy, and synergy are missing, there will be chaotic conditions. The organisation depends on the key individuals. It spends lot of time on fire fighting for issues and problems. There will be more blame games than solutions.

In the case of airline, the customer will experience delayed flights, poor in-flight service, and delayed delivery of checked-in luggage or missing luggage. Any ignorance of safety can result in disaster. The organisation can be having financial mess, and financial disaster is awaited due to lack of strategies.

- −Sm−Sg+St: There is a vision and a mission by top leaders; however, it is not supported either by systems or by the people. Leadership does not perform walk the talk.

  Airline has a strategy by selecting specific travel segment. Lack of system can result in inefficiencies in operation; for example, long time to get the boarding pass. In the lack of synergy elements, the customer will experience poor response by the airline staff.

- +Sm−Sg−St: The organisation has established a system by developing processes and acquiring tools. Leadership does not provide vision, and people do not have motivation to bring out their best. Work is done in a mechanical way, and growth is slow or stagnant.

  In the case of airline, the customer will see efficiencies in operation; for example, flight on time. However, the customer will not have a good experience with people.

- −Sm+Sg−St: People are friendly. However, the leadership lacks direction, and there are no systems to support. The customer's experience will be like a friendly open zoo.

  In the case of airline, the customer will experience friendly smile and nice talk. However, the request on flight service will not be responded properly due to lack of system.

- +Sm+Sg−St: The systems are present through processes and process automation. People are friendly and cooperative. However, the organisation has status quo and runs like maintenance function without growth.

  In the case of airline, growth is stagnant, and there is a lack of strategy, which also means lack of innovation. Customer and staff experience monotony and will not be delighted with innovation.

- +Sm−Sg+St: The systems are present, and management has strategy. There is competition among individuals and among the teams. This can result in barriers for each other and non-cooperation will impact on the results of the company.

  In the case of airline, different teams like ground staff, cabin crew team, and catering service team take care of different aspects.

Lack of coordination can lead to customer dissatisfaction. It can be lack of cleanliness in waiting area (lounge) or in cabin. Customers will not be happy.

- −Sm+Sg+St: Management has strategies, and people collaborate with each other. When systems are not supporting, there will be inefficiencies.

  In the case of airline, systems also mean use of information technology effectively and integration of systems. If system is not adequate to support frequent flier scheme, airline will not offer frequent flier and proper service and will not be able to attract and retain its customers.

- +Sm+Sg+St: This is the best combination. Organisation will have efficiency because of systems. Organisation will have effectiveness due to strategic thinking. Organisation will optimise the output through synergy.

  When airline has all these three—system, synergy, and strategy—in place, airline staff will be efficient, effective, and energetic. Customers will experience excellence in service and will become loyal customers. The customer retention will ensure profitability and sustainability. The supplier network to the airline will also get the business. Thus, the whole supply chain works well with quality programme supported with system, synergy, and strategy.

5.9 Porter's Value Chain

Porter gave another way to look at the organisation in terms of value chain. In Chapter 4, Section 4.5 (product life cycle and value cycle) discussed how the customer sees value in product (or service). The value chain shows the producer side, how value is created by producer organisation. An organisation can have two types of activities:

- Primary activity

  o Inbound logistics: Receiving, storing, and distributing inputs internally
  o Operation: Converting inputs into outputs sold to the customers
  o Output logistic: Distributing, storing, and delivering the product

  o   Marketing and sales: Persuading customer to buy the product
  o   Service: After-sale service

- Support activities (across all primary activities)

  o   Procurement: Vendor management and purchasing
  o   Human resources management: Recruiting, inducting, training, rewarding, and retaining people
  o   Technological development: Developing technology for product, process, information, and knowledge.
  o   Infrastructure: Support systems to maintain daily operations; for example, accounting, legal, administrative, general management and so on.

From a quality perspective, quality of activity will determine the value addition. As discussed, every activity and their integration can be analysed for—

- What are the systems provided?
- What are the strategies?
- What is the level of synergy?

Quality Management System can be seen from a value chain perspective.

5.10 Quality and Culture

Quality Management System will contribute towards building a quality culture. TQM gives a lot of emphasis on changing culture to quality culture. Most of the articles on TQM and Quality culture talk about values required for TQM. Values are important constituent of culture. TV Rao (in his book *Managers Who Make a Difference*) considers culture as a set of key principles and values that holds organisation together by providing standards for its members' behaviour. In short, it is values and behaviour.

Schein (in his model) suggests that culture exists at three levels:

- Assumptions—these are beliefs that are taken for granted
- Values—social principles or philosophies having intrinsic worth

- Artefacts—visible, tangible, and audible results of activity influenced by values and assumptions.

In short, it is beliefs, values, and behaviour. We have discussed their relationship in Section 5.4.

Geert Hofstede has an extensive research on organisational culture. According to him, an individual carries several layers (like onion). The core is values. Different levels can be viewed with quality aspects.

- National level: This is culture based on a person's country. Importance and perception of quality will be different for the Japanese, Indian, British, and American. Quality programme of multinational or global business needs to take care of this aspect.
- Regional and/or ethnic and/or religious and/or linguistic affiliation level: Countries like India and China have different cultures in different regions. The preferences may differ with regions. The quality strategy for marketing will differ.
- Gender level: Cultural difference can be due to bringing up as boys and girls. There can be different perceptions about quality. In the case of QMS promotion, we should take care of gender ratio.
- Social level: Culture can be influenced by profession and income group. The quality programme in accounting services will differ from the quality programme in manufacturing organisation.
- Generation level: Cold war generation and post-cold war generation will differ in their thinking and values. In the case of promoting QMS, we should take care of age groups or different generations.
- Organisation level: Organisations influence over the people. Leaders have the responsibility to set the tone and demonstrate values.

Geert Hofstede defined four dimensions, which are as follows:

- Power distance: It is about power distribution. Small power distance means more equality among all. Large power distance means towards inequality. Small power distance will encourage participation and contribute towards quality.
- Collectivism versus individualism: Collectivism is integrated cohesive group. Individualism focuses on the identity of the

individual. Harmony and consensus are useful qualities of collectivism to function as a team. Individualism has useful qualities like freedom and task focus. These help in giving candid feedback and accomplishing work.

- Feminine versus masculine: This dimension is about dominant values. Masculine is related to assertiveness, competitiveness, and performance orientation. Feminine is related to the quality of work life and equality.
- Uncertainty avoidance: This is the extent to which the members of a culture feel threatened by uncertain or unknown situations and try to avoid such situations. Weak uncertainty avoidance people will have less stress, feel comfortable in ambiguous situation and get motivated by achievement. High uncertainty avoidance people focus on precision and punctuality and are motivated by security.

Geert Hofstede discussed about the manifestation of culture in society.

- Rituals: Socially essential activity carried out for one's own sake. For example, different ways of greeting in different community.
- Heroes: Persons or imaginary characters having highly appreciated characteristics of culture.
- Symbols: Gesture, picture, objects that signifies specific meaning in culture.

Quality culture also needs to consider manifestation.

Based on experience in Japan, Dr W. Edwards Deming found that it takes twenty years to change a culture from an emphasis on productivity to an emphasis on quality (Reference CSQA CBOK). Quality programme is a long-term strategy and has longer payback period, considering cultural change.

Better approach to make a shift to quality culture can be—

- Make use of neurological levels, especially values and behaviour levels.
- Set policies to encourage and enforce new behaviour.
- Make continual improvement effective to pave the new quality culture.
- Manifest the quality culture.

5.11 Organisation Structure and Quality

Processes in QMS define RACI chart. RACI stands for responsible, accountable, consulted, and informed. RACI chart can provide good account of responsibility and accountability. On neurological level, organisation structure is a system at environment. At behaviour level (synergy aspects), it is about relationship. Hence, we can consider role, responsibilities, and relationship.

An organisation needs to have strategies, policies, and guidelines with reference to the organisation structure. These include level of authority or decision-making and also how delegation to subordinates and escalation to seniors work. The flexibility in the organisation structure is important for the successful quality programme.

Quality programme revolves around three things—quality control, quality assurance, and quality management. Quality control is about testing of product. This function provides lag indicators, which are known only after the product is produced. Quality assurance is about the process control. These are lead indicators showing that process is in control. In the case of quality control and quality assurance, independence is essential for candid reporting.

Quality management is coordination of continual improvements. This may require cross-functional teams, and facilitation is crucial to successful coordination.

5.12 Qualities of QMS

Quality Management System can be viewed from its usage.

- QMS has processes which answer how to perform certain activities. It serves as knowledge data. Employees can refer for know-how. Ease of navigation and ease in search are required.
- QMS has the knowledge and information. Hence, trainings can utilise QMS in preparing staff for the job.
- QMS processes are the baselines. This is useful on different aspects:

  o Capturing performance and compliance indicators
  o Automation of processes

o   Optimal use of resources
o   Further improvements

5.13 Resource Sucker

QMS should not become overheads and a bureaucratic hurdle. If it brings bureaucracy, then instead of optimal use of resources, it will consume resources. The following story of the cats and the monkey can illustrate this.

Two cats were fighting for a bar of butter. The first cat said, 'I saw the butter first, so I should get the maximum portion'. The second cat said, 'I am the one who reached the butter earlier. I deserve the bigger portion'. The first cat argued, 'I am the elder cat, so with high respect, give me the bigger portion'. The second cat said, 'You should be modest to give the younger cat the bigger portion'.

A monkey was watching both the cats. He stepped in and said, 'I have a balance to weigh. I can do justice and give you two the right proportion.' The cats agreed.

The monkey created two unequal parts and put them in balance. The left side of the balance went down. Being unequal, the monkey ate some portion from the bigger part on the left side. Now the right side of the balance went down. The monkey ate some more butter from right side of the balance. The left side of the balance went down. The monkey continued to eat the butter bar. Finally, the monkey said, 'You need to have a bigger butter bar for better butter distribution'.

5.14 In Summary

Quality Management System (QMS) needs to be viewed from a different perspective so that it becomes a holistic integrated system. Neurological levels are logical levels to organise QMS. QMS also needs to have system, synergy, and strategy.

QMS contents can be analysed based on wheel of life and value chain. Appropriate organisational structure and culture are required for QMS functioning.

SECTION 3:

Communication for Quality

6

Quality Language

My colleague once said, 'People are dull to meet a quality professional. The words like audit, non-conformance, failure rate, and defects scare them'. Language, the communication tool, needs quality to make the quality programme exciting.

Though this is the sixth chapter, we started the quality language from Chapter 1 itself, and it is to be used in all chapters. This chapter highlights the NLP in communication. Earlier sections of this chapter discuss positive language, clean language, and proactive language. Later sections discuss promoting quality through training, coaching, facilitating, and mentoring.

6.1 Communication Preferences VAK

We have preferences in how others should communicate to us. We have five senses: visual (what we see), auditory (what we listen), olfactory (what we smell), gustatory (what we taste), and kinaesthetic (what we experience by doing or our feelings). Predominantly, we have three communication preferences:

- Visual: These people like diagrams, graphs, charts, illustrations and so on. They will also use the word predominantly related to visualisation—

  o Show me the figures
  o Let us view the situation

- Auditory: These people love to hear stories, events, audio recording and so on. They will also use the word predominantly related to audio—

  o Tell me the figures
  o Let us hear about the situation

- Kinaesthetic: These people wish to perform the activity or exercise or get the feeling. They will also use the word predominantly related to feeling or action—

  o Get the feel of numbers
  o Let us sense the situation

Quality is often equated with documentation because well-defined processes mean processes have documentation. However, it is necessary to question how documentation connects a visual person, an auditory person, and a kinaesthetic person.

Today, we can easily have audio visual e-learning for processes. We can have quality management system with extensive use of audio visual.

6.2 Clean Language

Words have different meanings. If we look in the dictionary or click on thesaurus, we get several different meanings. For example, the word 'service' has different meanings—repair, tune, help, use, facility, ceremony and so on. A person stores his/her experience in the form of VAKOG (Visual, Auditory, Kinaesthetic, Olfactory, and Gustatory). When we listen or hear the word 'service', the meaning of service is as per the internal representation in our mind in the form of VAKOG (car repair, tuning computer for performance, help at the airport, facilities of the club, or service at church). Thus, it has different meaning for different persons. The communication happens at the conscious level as well as the unconscious level of our mind. Hence, we need to be careful in our language to provide the right meaning in the right spirit. This is possible through clean language and avoiding certain words. The words that can annoy and lead to different meanings are don't, but, and try. Let us explore how they affect.

Don't

This is commonly used in instructions. Manager says, 'Don't think about the errors.' The subordinate will think about the error(s) because the unconscious mind cannot process the negative instruction without focusing on the positive side.

During the presentation, if the presenter says, 'Do not look at the handouts. First listen to me', invariably, the audience will have temptation to look at the handouts.

As a part of clean language, we need to avoid the use of 'don't' and give instruction in positive words.

But

This word negates everything said before it. For example, if a manager says, 'Your performance is excellent, but . . .' This means the subordinate understands it as not excellent. Similarly, when the subordinate is speaking with the manager and he (or she) says, 'I agree with you, but . . . ', the manager will interpret it as disagreement. The solution to this is to use 'and' instead of 'but'. For example, 'I agree with you, and it is better to have . . .' This will lead to agreement.

Try

This is another word that is close to saying 'no'. When a manager asks, 'When will this job be complete?', the subordinate answers, 'I will try to complete by next week'. 'Try' means work is done half-heartedly and will not be complete. It is good to avoid the word 'try' and be firm on doing or completing the task.

Thus, to practice clean language, we should avoid 'don't', 'but', and 'try'. First, we can monitor the usage of these words and then practice to avoid.

6.3 Positive Language

As per direction filter (NLP Meta Programmes), people are motivated by two ways—one is achieving the target and avoiding the failure. We discussed motivation in Chapter 1.

Let us discuss perception filter, question, and options to check the preference is—

- What do you want in job?

    o Towards (optimist)
    o Towards with little away
    o Both towards and away equally (realist)
    o Away with little towards
    o Away (pessimist)

The two polarities are: 'Towards' and 'Away'. Towards people use these words and are motivated by these words:

- Achieve, attain, have, accomplish
- Benefits, advantages
- Enables

Away people use these words and are motivated by these words:

- Avoid, fix, prevent
- To deal with
- To get rid of
- Imperfect, wrong, problems

Profession also impacts the preferences. Medical profession can be more 'away' type. Marketing professional will tend to be 'towards' type. Quality professionals are also seen as 'Away' type person. Sometimes, the quality programme is also influenced 'away' language.

The 'away' language is negative. The common expectation from quality professional is to detect mistakes or look at the failures. Hence, at the end of audit, quality auditor reports the non-conformances. At the end of software testing, the tester will login test incidents. The feedback given by auditor or tester is good. The away person gets satisfied with not having bad report. Absence of failure need not be an excellence. Absence of failure may lead to absence of experimenting. In experimenting, we learn from failures. In reality, many organisations learn from failures and reach the excellence.

Positive language looks at achievement or accomplishment. The negative statement can be converted into positive statement. For example, the aim is to reduce the failure rate. This can be expressed such as to increase the success rate. Instead of saying 'we have a problem', we can say, 'we have a challenge'.

It is important to look at the positive intention of the activity and express it in a positive manner. There is an NLP presupposition:

- Behind every **behaviour** is a positive intention.

  OR

- All **behaviour** has positive intention.

If intention at lower level is seen in a negative manner, we need to ask the higher-level intention. For example, testing means to detect defect and to demonstrate the fitness for use (Reference: ISTQB Glossary of terms). The errors encountered will be reported by the tester. The developer feels the errors are direct reflection of his work. He or she takes it personally (unconscious mind also takes personally!) If we look at higher intention, it is to deliver quality system or product. This is same for the developer and the tester. It is important to mention the purpose in a positive manner.

6.4 Proactive Language

Before looking at proactive language, it is good to understand the term proactive. As per action filter (NLP Meta Programme), a person has preferences in responding to the situation. This shows the person's energy to act. The question and options to check the preference are as follows:

- When you come into a situation, do you usually act quickly after sizing it up, or do you do a detailed study?

  o   Proactive
  o   Sometimes proactive, sometimes reactive
  o   Reactive
  o   Inactive

The proactive nature can be analysed based on two parameters: reflection and action. The four combinations are shown in figure 6.1.

		Reflection	
		Reflective	Non-reflective
Action	Active	Proactive	Reactive
	Inactive	Passive (Procrastination)	Meditative

Figure 6.1 Action parameters

When there is no thinking and no action, it is meditative state. This state is good for relaxation.

When there is thinking and no action, it is passive state. This is useful for handling risky situation with thorough thinking. However, it is undesirable if it leads to procrastination.

When there is no thinking and only body action, it is reaction. This will be very useful in situation like sports or near-miss incident. In the case of cricket, if you are a close in fielder, you need to react quickly to catch the ball. Someone reacts quickly to avoid accident, and it becomes near-miss incident.

When there is thinking and action, it is proactive. Stephen Covey has defined the proactive model in his book *The 7 Habits of Highly Effective People*. The response without thinking is reactive response. The response with thinking is proactive response.

Stephen Covey has given the examples of reactive language and proactive language in his book. Table 6.1 shows reactive and proactive responses.

Reactive Language	Proactive Language
• There is nothing I can do.	• Let us look at our alternatives.
• That's just the way I am.	• I can choose a different approach.
• He makes me so mad.	• I control my own feelings.
• They won't allow that.	• I can create an effective presentation.

Table 6.1 Proactive response

6.5 People's Preference for Information

Communication means giving and getting information and processing it. People have preference as to how the information is given to them. They also have a preferred way of processing it.

Let us look at the chunk size filter with a question and options.

Question: If you were going to start using QMS, what would you like to know?

- Big picture, global, abstract
- Big picture then details, global to specific (Deductive)
- Details then big picture, specific to global (Inductive)
- Details, specific

The two polarities are 'Big picture' and 'Details'. The big picture people will be happy when we provide summary or abstract or when we present a concept. After understanding the big picture, these people can accept the information randomly. The details people will be happy when we provide a step-by-step process in a sequential manner. In the case of QMS, the documents should be available at both levels—conceptual level and specifics level. QMS will satisfy both types of people.

Let us look at the relationship filter which indicates the way of understanding and deciding. The question and options are as follows:

Question: How will you develop understanding of QMS and adopting changes?

- Sameness
- Sameness with exception
- Differences with exception
- Differences

The two polarities are 'Sameness' and 'Differences'. The sameness people will be happy when we tell processes or systems that are unchanged or same as before. The differences people will be happy when we tell them systems or processes are new and totally different or systems or processes have a complete turnaround. In the case of QMS, we need to make changes, and it is challenging to communicate the changes. Considering both—sameness and difference people—information should have both orientations (that is same → new or new → same). The convincing of change is discussed in Chapter 11.

6.6 Promoting Quality

Promotion of quality management system needs careful planning and strategy. It requires mix of training, coaching, mentoring, and facilitating. Continual improvement also leads to continual learning (also known as lifelong learning). Figure 6.2 shows the different ways of learning and development.

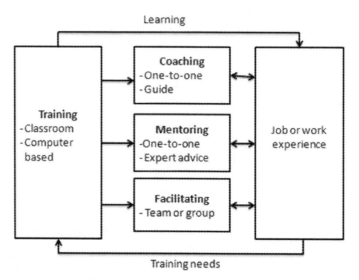

Figure 6.2 Relation among learning and development tools

Some organisations have clear strategy and system for learning development (for example, 10 per cent training, 20 per cent coaching/ mentoring/facilitating, and 70 per cent work experience). When these are in sync, the organisation can have synergy in learning and development. Each tool has been discussed in subsequent sections.

6.7 Training

Trainings are required during the introduction of QMS, and also, ongoing trainings are required for changes to the QMS. The change management is discussed in Chapter 11. Communication is the key for change management, and trainings form a major part of communication for change. Training has responsibility to spread quality language (clean, positive, and proactive). There are more tips from NLP for training.

Bernice McCarthy developed the 4-Mat system, which combines various learning style into one system. The 4-Mat system has been widely used for training design. The four quadrants of the 4-Mat system are as follows:

- First quadrant (why and why not?): This should explain all the benefits and advantages of QMS. The trainees should realise their needs and how QMS addresses those needs. This is an interactive session that motivates and witnesses. In this part of training, we can use all learning from Chapter 1, especially McCleland's motivators and Tony Robbins's motivators. In addition, Chapter 3 discussed the benefits as a part business case; we can highlight the benefits of QMS covered in business case. Trainees can brainstorm to account for the different needs and benefits.
- Second quadrant (what about it?): This should explain the terms and concepts. For example, every quality framework has different processes. Each process has objectives, terms, concepts, roles and responsibilities, activities, records, metrics and so on. Incident management process has terms like incident, urgency, impact, priority and so on. The aim of this quadrant is to provide information. If PowerPoint slides are prepared, we need to ensure the chunk size in each slide (that is maximum six points in a slide and maximum six words for each point). We can use relevant diagrams, metaphors, stories, and exercises to enhance the training and help the trainees understand better. Trainees can learn theories with their ability to analyse and classify.
- Third quadrant (how does it work?): This is a demonstration of a process or system. We need to provide step-by-step instructions. For complex processes, it is good to break into activities (smaller chunks). We can use diagrams for easier illustrations. We can provide additional explanation for steps. This may be repeating the concepts given in quadrant two. The trainer will act as a coach for this quadrant. Trainees will learn more by experimenting and altering.

- Fourth quadrant (what if): After the demo, the trainees will have hands-on experience. This will be self-discovery. At the end, the trainees will share the experience. The trainer will conduct a question-and-answer session and clarify the doubts. Trainees will learn more through creativity and risking.

The 4-Mat system is shown diagrammatically in Figure 6.3. The 4-Mat system also encompasses four different learning styles: learning by reflecting is through 'Why' and 'What' (that is quadrant 1 and 2), learning by thinking is through 'What' and 'How' (that is quadrant 2 and 3), learning by doing is through 'How' and 'What if' (that is quadrant 3 and 4), and learning by experience is through 'What if' and 'Why' (that is quadrant 4 and 1). QMS trainings must be holistic from a learning perspective, and the 4-Mat system helps to make the trainings holistic.

Quadrant 4: Question: What if...? Answer: Let them learn themselves using hands-on	Quadrant 1: Question: Why (and why not?) Answer: Provide reasons and relevance
Quadrant 3: Question: How does it work? Answer: Coach them on process.	Quadrant 2: Question: What about it? Answer: Give more information

Figure 6.3 The 4-Mat system

Another aspect of training is to consider the left brain and right brain. Left brain is related to logical, sequential, rational, analytical, and objective thinking. Right brain is related to random, intuitive, holistic, synthesising, and subjective thinking. Our educational system, work systems, and training programmes are more focused on the left brain. However this does not mean that a person who is left or right-brain dominated does not use the other part of his brain. For most people, the two parts of the brain work in tandem to enable them to function as well-rounded personalities. In order to be more 'whole-brained' in our orientation, training programmes need to give equal weight to the arts, creativity, and the skills of imagination and synthesis.

6.8 Coaching

When executives, especially senior executives, are busy and have difficulty in sparing time for training hours (or days), option can be coaching.

Coaching also plays complementary role for training. Coaching may follow trainings. Many organisation look forwards to managers to act as a coach for their subordinates. Some people think coaching is required for underperformance. However, coaching is to support the achievement of business outcome by enabling systematic change.

Quality management programme aims at continual improvements. This requires setting goals and bringing a desired change in a desired timeframe. Coaching is a process and not an advice. The coach guides through the process, and the client learns through self-discovery. Coaching is done for limited period (sessions) with specific purpose. The steps in GROW model used in coaching is as follows:

- Goal Setting: The first step is to define the goals. The goals should be specific, measurable, attainable, realistic, and time-bound. (SMART goal setting is discussed in detail in Chapter 7.) These goals could be business goals or goals of executive.
- Reality Check: After defined goals, the gap is defined by checking the current status and desired status. The most common factors that will make or break the success of achieving the goal are as follows:

  o Knowledge: Lack of knowledge can be addressed by trainings.
  o Skills: Skill development can happen through mentoring and on-the-job experience.
  o Attitude: This is related to values and beliefs. This is discussed in Chapter 5.
  o Aptitude: It is a natural talent or ability (physical and mental) which can be innate or acquired through education, training, and life experience. It is a mix of natural and nurtured skills.

- Options: These are different means or ways of achieving goal. Options need resources and will have certain risks associated. Resources can be financial, physical, time, and mental. Risk management covers solution for the constraints, weakness, and threats.

- **Wrap-up**: We need to have a clear finishing line. This gives clarity on achievement of goal. For every session, wrap-up covers review of progress and way ahead.

A coach should be good at listening skills, building rapport, giving feedback, and motivating for result.

6.9 Mentoring

Mentoring also works on a one-to-one basis. A mentor is an experienced person with a considerable degree of subject knowledge. Mentorship programme is long-term and has broad scope related to work. Unlike coaching, session can be informal. The mentor takes care of the following:

- Offers opportunities for skill development
- Identifies the gap in skills
- Provide helpful advice
- Be a role model
- Encourage people to think for themselves

The mentee takes the following responsibilities:

- Has willingness to learn and devotes time
- Accepts advice and feedback positively
- Ready to stretch for the results
- Becomes a successor

Organisation may have a pool of mentors with different expertise.

6.10 Facilitating

Coaching and mentoring is on individual basis. The team and groups work on various quality initiatives. The facilitator plays key role in the following discussions or meeting:

- Brainstorming session
- Problem-solving discussion

- Handling challenging situations in a meeting
- Conflict resolution
- Decision making with consensus

Key skills for the facilitator are as follows:

- Presentation skills to present the topic in a clear and concise manner
- Listening skills
- Observation skills to understand body language
- Creating conducive environment and encouraging participation
- Controlling discussion and managing time
- Summarising the discussion and helping the team to arrive at conclusion
- Organising the meeting

6.11 Learning from Work Experience

We learn through training, coaching, and mentoring. All learning turned into actions at work. It enriches us with more learning through practical aspects and handling different situations. With the knowledge of NLP, we can look at the following aspects:

- How do I store and remember my experience in terms of VAKOG? (that is visual, auditory, kinaesthetic, olfactory, and gustatory) More details on internal representation are in Appendix A.
- What are the strategies in decision-making? Strategy (NLP term) is explained in Chapter 8.
- What are my behaviours? How do I look forwards to modelling (from role model)? Modelling (NLP term) is discussed in Chapter 4.

6.12 In Summary

The quality of our lives is determined by the quality of our communication. Quality management programme is not an exception. Quality programme needs to be supported with training, coaching, facilitating, and mentoring.

Quality language also makes a difference. Quality programme should use proactive, positive, and clean language.

SECTION 4:

Business and Quality

7

Project Management

Project Management is a necessity for every organisation when organisation wants to implement new ideas or establish new process. Project Management is an interdisciplinary management tool used across different industries. Construction industry is highly project intensive, whereas banking services will not have projects as a core activity. However, all organisations will take up quality improvement projects. Successful execution of those projects will provide required breakthroughs.

NLP can help in project management. This chapter discusses project management briefly and provides NLP tools.

7.1 Project Management Book of Knowledge (PMBOK)

Project Management Institute (PMI, USA) is a leading professional organisation. PMI provides up-to-date knowledge and frameworks for project management through its PMBOK. PMBOK has forty-seven processes across five process groups (initiating, planning, executing, controlling, and closing) and in ten knowledge areas (Integration Management, Scope Management, Time [schedule] Management, Cost Management, Quality Management, Human Resources Management, Communication Management, Risk Management, Procurement Management, and Stakeholder Management).

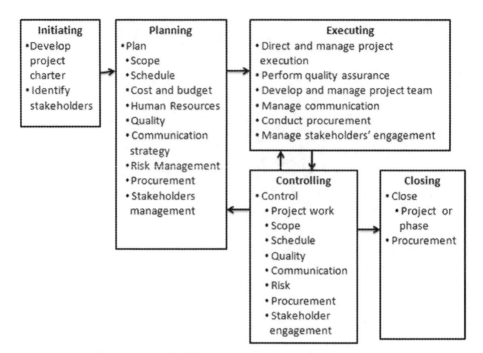

Figure 7.1 PMBOK Process groups and major process

Major processes of PMBOK process groups are shown in Figure 7.1.

7.2 PRINCE 2 (Project IN Controlled Environment Version 2)

UK Government agency office of Government Commerce developed PRINCE 2, which is a popular project management methodology. It has seven processes (starting up a project, initiating a project, directing a project, controlling a stage, managing stage boundaries, managing product delivery, and closing a project) on the basis of seven principles (continued business justification, learn from experience, defined roles and responsibilities, manage by stages, manage by exception, focus on products, and tailored to suit the project environment) using seven themes (business case, organisation, quality, plans, risk, change, and progress).

Figure 7.2 shows the processes, principles, and themes of Prince 2.

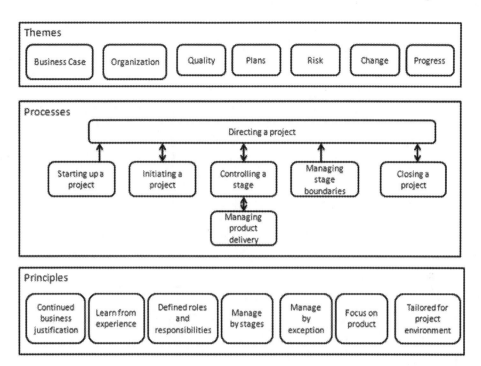

Figure 7.2 PRINCE 2—processes, principles and themes

7.3 Agile Project Management

Project duration varies. Long-term projects could be three years and short-term project could be three weeks. Question arises, should we use the same project management methodology for both projects or should we have a different methodology as per the duration of the project. Traditional project management puts lot of overheads for the short-term projects. Hence, short-term projects, especially software projects, prefer agile project management. Agile project management has iterative approach.

There are new terms in agile project management. Figure 7.3 shows the agile project management.

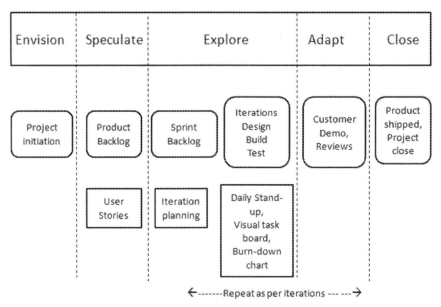

Figure 7.3 Agile project management

The phases in agile project management:

- Envision: Project is initiated. Project team is formed. Project objectives and constraints are defined.
- Speculate: Project planning is done. Broad requirements, including non-functional requirements, are gathered. This forms a product backlog. Iterative high-level release plan is prepared.
- Explore: This is about design, build, and test. There will be planning. This will have sprint backlog (term from Scrum that is, a type of agile project development). Requirements are user stories. The monitoring is through daily stand-up meeting, visual task board, and burn-down chart (remaining work in sprint backlog)
- Adapt: This includes reviews, customer demonstration, and project status check.
- Close: Releases as per plan.

7.4 Project Management Processes

More details are available in various books on processes defined in PMBOK and Prince 2 and also books on agile project management methodology.

Organisation should develop own processes for project management as per need.

As per Chapter 5, we need to check for systems, strategy, and synergy. System includes processes and tools. Strategy gives the options and flexibility in handling the project of different sizes and types. Synergy in project team is the people aspects to be addressed.

7.5 SMART Goal Setting

Project charter is initial document. Project charter defines the project objectives and may include major deliverables. Project plan is a formal approved document that helps in execution and control of the project. The project plan will have refined requirements, and project objectives and project deliverables get more clarity. The project can have phases and milestones. The objectives and deliverables are defined for phases and milestones.

Project management deals with three parameters:

- Cost: Have total cost of resources—human resources and physical resources as per budget.
- Time: Completing work on as per schedule.
- Scope: Provide deliverables as per requirements to achieve project objective.

To have clarity on objectives, it is good to use SMART goal setting. Let us consider a project to implement financial accounting system.

- **S**pecific and **s**imple: Specific means specify the functions of the system. Simple means not too detailed. Specifies what and not detailed how.
- **M**easurable and **m**eaningful (to stakeholder): Function will have performance-improvement objectives. This can be reduced cycle time or increased output. This should be measurable. For example, financial transaction processed per day. Stakeholders have the motivation to achieve these objectives. Faster financial transaction processing will improve efficiency of team by 50 per cent. If the cycle time reduction results in idle capacity, stakeholders may not be interested.

- **A**ttainable and **a**s if now: People working on a project must have the capability and potential to execute the project successfully, provide the deliverables, and achieve the objectives. The objectives are not defined in future tense. The implication is that people (and their subconscious) think it will be achieved in future. We need to achieve objectives at the end of the project.
- **R**ealistic and **r**esponsible: Realistic means feasibility check. There will be some uncertainty element in project. People should have technical ability and innovative ideas to provide creative solution. Responsibility is clarity on where the buck stops. Every project team should know their responsibility.
- **T**ime-bound and **t**owards stakeholders want: All objectives have to have target dates. Projects will have critical path and dependency on various activities. Project team works towards on time delivery. NLP defines requirements as 'away' and 'towards'. If we want to move away from failures, it is 'away' requirement. If we want to move towards success, it is 'towards' requirement. Hence, instead of saying reducing failure rate by 10 per cent, objective is stated as increasing success rate by 10 per cent. This gives positive approach to our thinking and to the project.

If the project deliverable is the financial accounting system, then the objectives are the benefits achieved by the project.

SMART project objective will reduce/remove ambiguity. For example, ambiguous objective is 'to reduce time to respond to complaints in the coming summer' By using SMART goal setting, it is 'to have response time faster by 30 per cent to the customer complaints by improving issue tracking system by DD/MMM/YYYY for example 11 Jun 2013.

7.6 Meta Model for Clarity

Communication is critical to project success. It may be managing scope (requirements) or understanding the user stories or a part of communication planning and controlling. NLP helps in bringing clarity. As per NLP communication model (refer appendix A), deletion, distortion, and generalisation happen during the communication. This results in miscommunication. Meta Model provides questions to ask so that information gets clarity. Here are some examples from IT system project:

- Deletion

  - Simple deletion: Statement—'Data files are received by email'. Question—'From whom, to whom, when, and what format?'
  - Simple deletion (Unspecified relationship): Statement—'The resources in abundance for the project ensure project success'. Question—'What is the relationship between resources in abundance and successful projects?'
  - Comparative deletion: Statement—'Users have more test cases'. Question—'More than what? Which specific areas?'
  - Lack of referential index: Statement—'The users need this system feature'. Question—'Which user? Which feature?'
  - Unspecified verb: Statement—'System will perform calculations'. Question—'Which calculations and how?'
  - Nominalisation: Statement—'There is no security'. Question—'Which security—data security or system security or physical security or confidentiality?'

- Distortion

  - Mind reading: Statement—'IT department does not think about business'. Question—'How do you know IT department does not think about business?'
  - Lost performance: Statement—'It is bad to disobey the process standards'. Question—'Who says it is bad? For whom it is bad? How do you know that'
  - Complex equivalence: Statement—'I clicked save button and the computer hanged'. Question—'How does saving make a computer hanged?'
  - Cause and effect: Statement—'If only a few bugs are detected in testing, there will be more failure in production system'. Question—'How do bugs during testing determine the failures of system in production?'
  - Presupposition: Statement—'If IT department knows the user, the user will not suffer'. Question—'How does user

choose to suffer? How do you know IT department does not know the user?'

- Generalisation

    - Universal quantifier: Statement—'Always draw a flow chart before coding'. Question—'Always? Do all coding need a flow chart?'
    - Modal operator (possibility): Statement—'He cannot test this issue'. Question—'What prevents him?'
    - Modal operator (necessary): Statement—'He must use ten test cases for each option for data entry'. Question—'What would happen if he did not?'

7.7 Time-based Technique

Would you like to move into past and future? It is possible through imagination. We can imagine a line of time and walk on that line. The exercises in this section are to be done under the supervision of a certified NLP practitioner. Before walking into the future, let us get familiar with different lines for time.

We can ask a person, 'How do you see past, present, and future?' We can give two options as shown in Figures 7.4 and 7.5.

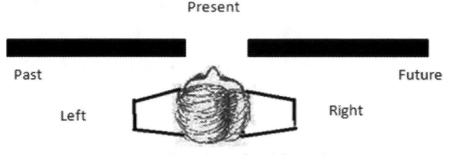

Figure 7.4 Timeline is from left to right

A person may have a timeline from left to right that is, left is past, present is at the centre, and future is on the right. Someone may have the choice to have past in the right and future on the left. In NLP terms, these persons have 'Through-Time' timeline.

A person may have a timeline from back to front that is, back is past, present at the centre, and future is front. Someone may have the choice to have past in the front and future in the back. In NLP terms, these persons have 'In-Time' Timeline.

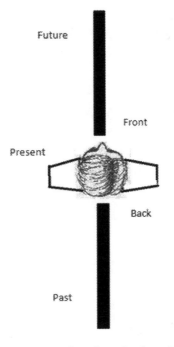

Figure 7.5 Timeline from back to front

This classification has some peculiarities associated with them. A through-time person has time in front, plans activity well, and likes to do work as per plan. An in-time person lives in the present, focuses on the task in hand, and usually works hard towards the deadline.

Let us look at the use of time-based technique in project management.

Let us consider an 'in-time' person seeing the future in the front. The person is working on a project with two milestones (intermediate goals) and final completion (project goal). He needs work on task and with people. Project will have some elements of uncertainty as well as risk. If his mind works towards successful achievement of milestones and successful outcome of the project, there are higher chances of achieving the success. The mind does not differentiate between reality and imagination. With imagination, we can experience the future and use that experience in project execution.

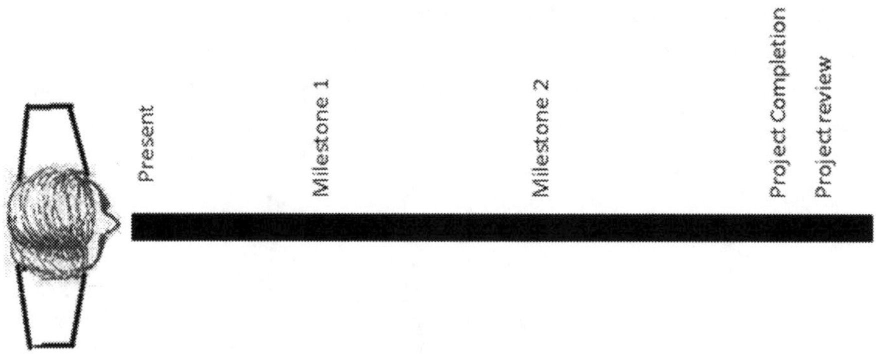

Figure 7.6 Timeline with project schedule

An NLP practitioner can conduct the session. The project team member will stand at the position, and it is marked as present. The practitioner will instruct the following:

- Imagine future timeline in the front (consider the space available in the room).
- Tell me where you see the project completion on this line.
- Practitioner marks the position and keeps object (for example, pen or memento).
- Are there any milestones for this project? As shown in Figure 7.6, there are two milestones.
- Practitioner marks the milestones.
- Project team member writes the action plan for milestones and project.
- With this action plan, what is the rating you would like to give for successfully achieving project objective(s)? Project team member will provide rating on scale of 0 to 10.
- Project team member walks slowly on the timeline and imagines the execution of project. Reaches the first milestone.
- On achieving milestone 1,

  o What are your feelings?
  o What are the learning? (note down the points)
  o What are the changes to action plan?
  o What is the rating for successful completion?

- Project team member walks slowly on the timeline and imagines the execution of project. Reaches the second milestone.
- On achieving milestone 2,

  o What are your feelings?
  o What are the learning? (note down the points)
  o What are the changes to action plan?
  o What is the rating for successful completion?

- Project team member walks slowly on the timeline and imagines the execution of project. Reaches the project completion.
- On completing,

  o What are your feelings?

- A week later, there is post-project review.

  o What are the learning? What are the takeaways from this project?

- Project team member walks back to present position.
- Project team member can relook at—

  o Motivation and feel of achievement
  o Detailed action plan with additional learning
  o With this, check the improvement in success rating of the project.

The memento kept on the timeline to mark the project completion is given to the project team member. It acts as a reminder or an anchor to work on the project and complete it successfully.

7.8 Perceptual Positions

Perceptual position is a tool to understand the different perspectives. In projects, the project team needs to understand the requirements of the stakeholders. As a part of quality control, verification or reviews are conducted. Project team can use perceptual position to prepare for the meetings with customer and meetings for review. Every person has his or her own map of the world. Hence, we see things differently, and hence, it is good to see different perspectives for better communication.

Prior to meetings (or important meeting), the project team can exercise perceptual positions. NLP practitioner can conduct a session for this exercise.

- First position (own shoe/our own map of the world): This is the project team member(s)' perspective:

    o How do you behave and feel about the project?
    o What is important to you? What do you want from this project?
    o What are the action points for this project?

Write down the answers to these questions. The first question addresses the mental resources (for example, confidence, assertive, composed and so on) Second question will give thought on the motivation. Third question provides action plan.

- Second position (their shoe/their map of the world): This can be customer giving the requirements or reviewer giving the feedback. Now move to second point which represents customer or reviewer and answer the same questions.

    o How do you behave and feel?
    o What is important to you? What do you want?
    o What is there to learn? What are the changes to your perception?

Write down the answers and get complete picture from others' perspective.

- Combine both answer sets to have a better understanding of the project and better action plan.

If we wish to take an independent view, we can add a third position and get more learning for improved action plan.

We can combine perceptual with time based technique. Figure 7.6 is modified with perceptual position. It is shown in Figure 7.7.

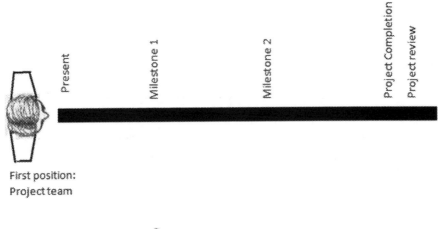

First position:
Project team

Second position:
Customer

Figure 7.7 Perceptual positions

7.9 The Bricklayers' Story

Significance of project and quality work happens if the project team has a big picture of the project.

Once a king was building a huge castle. He appointed architects, bricklayers, and artisans. The bricklayers were laying bricks.

The king visited that construction site. He asked the first bricklayer, 'What are you doing?'

The first bricklayer said, 'I am laying bricks.'

The king asked the same question to the second bricklayer.

The second bricklayer said, 'I am building a wall.'

The king asked the same question to the third bricklayer.

The third bricklayer said, 'I am building a castle.'

The king smiled.

7.10 In Summary

Every business needs project management. Project needs human resources and physical resources. The human resources need resourceful state of mind and sound communication among the project stakeholder. Project

131

management processes are available with various project management frameworks and models. NLP tools can complement the project management processes and supercharge the project team.

SMART goal setting brings clarity on project objectives and project deliverables.

Perceptual positions can provide better understanding of different stakeholders.

Meta model provides the questioning to reduce the impact of deletion, distortion, and generalisation in communication. These questions expand the project team's model of the world (to understand the model of the world of different stakeholders) and bring the clarity.

Time-based technique improves overall motivation for the project and probability of successful project execution.

8

Service Management

Service is becoming a significant component of business. Service may be with tangible goods (like after-sales service for costly equipments) or it is major services with minor goods (like doctor providing medical service and medicine) or it is pure services (like consulting). Service may be to the internal customer or external customer. In other words, all human interaction in business can be linked to service. Service management needs to be established to provide service quality experience to service consumer.

ITIL defines service management as a set of specialised organisational capabilities for providing value to the customer in the form of services.

This chapter explores model related to service. NLP concepts useful to service are discussed.

8.1 Bicycle Model

Wilson Learning developed bicycle model for service management. It provides excellent analogy. It combines technical skills and soft skills or people skills. Let us look at four dimensions as shown in Figure 8.1.

- Front wheel: This represents people skills. These include courtesy, empathy, and friendliness. This is supported by patience and good communication skill. The front wheel balances the back wheel and guides. People skills similarly complement technical skills.
- Back wheel: This represents technical skills. These include technical knowledge, business knowledge, product knowledge, process knowledge, and knowledge about policies and compliance. The

back wheel provides the power; similarly, technical skills provide the power to service delivery.

Figure 8.1 Bicycle model for service management

- Gears: This represents the flexibility. This is the ability to shift between technical dimension and people dimension as per the customer's requirements. As per NLP presupposition, the person with the most flexibility in their behaviours will have greater influence over others. The ability to shift gears gives the ability to control the situation.
- Handlebars: This represents self-management. This is the ability to manage the own emotional response to direct the interaction towards positive. This is the ability to manage customer interaction successfully to give a positive experience to the customer.

In addition to this, we can consider two more things: paddling and carrier. The paddling speed represents the time to response and time to resolve. The carrier represents the capacity to take load or volume.

8.2 Gap Model of Service Quality

Parasuraman, Zeithaml, and Berry developed this model. Customer satisfaction depends on the gap between expectation and experience of actual service.

The five gaps are as follows:

- Gap between consumer's expectation and perception of service provider about consumer's expectation: This is an understanding of customer's or consumer's needs. It is effectiveness of market research or capturing the requirements.
- Gap between service provider's perception about consumer's expectation and service specification: The service is to be designed based on customer requirements. If service standards do not match the service requirements, then there will be a gap.
- Gap between the service specification and service provided: This is the lack of conformance to the standards, resulting in performance gap.
- Gap between service provided and service communicated: This is the communication gap between promises made by sales people and actual service provided. The promises also impact the consumer's expectation.
- Gap between consumer's perception of service provided and consumer's expectation: This is the net customer satisfaction. It is accumulation of other four gaps.

This model can be diagrammatically shown in Figure 8.2. Key point in this model is proper communication at every stage. Over-promise and underperformance can lead to poor customer satisfaction.

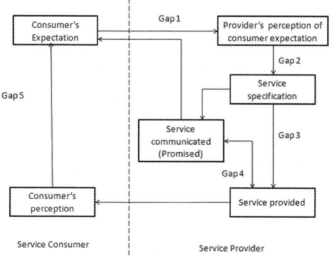

Figure 8.2 Gap model

8.3 Attribute Service Quality Model

Haywood-Framer developed attribute model for service quality. Three attributes are as follows:

- Physical facility and processes: This includes location, layout, range of services, size, process flow (speed) and flexibility and so on.
- Behavioural aspects: This includes communication (verbal and non-verbal), tone of voice, courtesy, warmth, friendliness, attentive, timeliness, neatness, smartly dressed and so on.
- Professional judgement: Competence, problem diagnosis and solution, guidance, advice, knowledge, innovation and so on.

Services need all three attributes at varying degrees. Ignoring any one attribute can lead to poor customer satisfaction and can result in going out of business. Service can be viewed from two elements—interaction intensity and customisation. (Model has third element is degree of labour. To simplify, we can consider two elements) Four combinations are—

- Low interaction intensity and low customisation: This has more significance of the first attribute—physical facility and processes. Examples of this type of service are grocery shop, public transport and so on.
- High interaction intensity and low customisation: This has more significance of behavioural aspects. The examples of this type of service are education or standardised training programmes.
- Low interaction intensity and high customisation: This has more significance of professional judgement (high customisation). The examples of this type of service are fitness club or tailor-made holiday package (free and easy).
- High interaction intensity and high customisation: This has more significance of professional judgement. The examples of this type of service are medical centre, legal service and so on.

8.4 Service Management Processes

ITIL processes provide the best practices for IT service management and also provide details of processes. These processes can be applicable to other services also. Besides continual service improvement, four phases are—

- Service strategy: This is to build organisational capability and create strategic assets for service.
- Service design: This is design and development of services.
- Service transition: This is to implement new and changed services into operation.
- Service operation: This is to have efficiency and effectiveness in operation.

Organisation should develop own processes for service management as per need.

As per Chapter 5, we need to check for systems, strategy, and synergy. System includes processes and tools. Strategy gives the options and flexibility. Synergy in service teams is how the people aspects are to be addressed.

8.5 NLP in Service Management

We looked at three models for service quality. NLP can help in people aspects of these models and also in establishing the processes for service management.

Communication preferences of people have been covered in Chapter 6. As per NLP presupposition, the meaning of the communication is the response you get. During the service interaction, we need to understand the client's model of the world and get clarity on issue or incident or the service request requirements.

Empathy means understanding the client's model of the world and respecting his or her model of the world. This will put the person in the client's shoe and give good service experience.

Two key NLP aspects (Rapport and Strategy) are discussed in the subsequent sections.

8.6 Rapport Building

As per NLP presuppositions, resistance in client is due to lack of rapport. In service engagement, in the very first interaction, we will prefer to establish rapport. Rapport helps to build trust and confidence in customer. This is good for both to have more productive time.

Traditional or non-NLP approach will advocate smile, eye-contact or handshake as part of rapport building. However, NLP suggests technique that engages a person's unconscious mind. Rapport needs to be built across all communication channels—in person or over the phone or through email.

Mantra of NLP for Rapport is 'Really All People Prefer Others Resembling Themselves.' Customer looks for commonality with the service desk person (or service provider). The commonality could be verbal or non-verbal. As the communication happens 55 per cent through body language, 38 per cent through vocal qualities, and 7 per cent through words, rapport also has the same percentage.

As per NLP, mind and body are linked through language. Mind reflects on body (physiology) and vice versa. When we match our body language with the body language of the other person, our thinking also matches and thus rapport is built. Physiology covers posture (sitting or standing) and gestures (facial expression, eye contact, breathing and so on). In case of service in person or meetings in person, it is useful to match body language.

Voice quality covers tone (high pitch or low pitch), tempo (fast or slow), and volume (loud or soft). This is applicable to service in person as well as service over the phone or conference call.

In case of emails, we can check for wording (that is, linguistic predicates. Refer Chapter 6, Section 6.1). If the computer system is not working, a person's reporting of the incident may provide a clue of the customer's preferred communication.

- I observed problem in the system (Visual)
- It sounds like system is having problem (Auditory)
- I experienced problem with the system (Kinaesthetic)

For replying email or during the correspondence, we can use similar wording to establish rapport through email.

Two important concepts are 'matching and mirroring' and 'pacing and leading'.

Matching and mirroring

Matching means doing exactly the same thing. If the first person touches his cheek with left hand and the second person touches his cheek with left hand, then the second person is matching. If the first person touches his cheek with left hand and the second person touches his cheek with right hand (mirror image), then the second person is mirroring. Matching and mirroring is not mimicry. It is done in a subtle way and in a discrete manner (with delay of few seconds) to express an empathy through body language. Figure 8.3 shows matching and mirroring.

Figure 8.3 Matching and mirroring

Pacing and leading

Pacing a person means following a person using matching or mirroring. For example, person A (kinaesthetic) will match person B (auditory) through physiology and/or vocal quality and/or words with person B's representation system—auditory. This will establish rapport between A and B. This means both persons A and B are in sync at subconscious level.

Second part is leading. In this example, it is assumed that person A knows how persons A and B wish to achieve outcome. Once the rapport is established, person A will start using his representation system (kinaesthetic), and person B starts following. In other words, person A is now leading. Thus, person A can convince person B in achieving the desired outcome.

In case of service interaction, the service desk officer (service provider) needs to establish rapport (i.e., pacing/mirroring and matching) to understand an incident or a request and lead him/her/them to the solution.

8.7 Cues for Understanding Customer

It is important for the service provider to make out preferred system of communication and thought process of the customer. In NLP, it is called sensory acuity. Different cues are just indicators and are not rigid rules.

Linguistic predicates

We have seen preferred representation system in Chapter 6 (Section 6.1). We need to develop observation skills to make out their preferred representation system (auditory, visual, or kinaesthetic) further; we can also make out their strategy (next Section 8.8). We need to notice their language or the linguistic predicates used to understand the preferred representation system.

Physiological cues

We may be able to recognise the representational system by observing physiology.

Let us look at the postures and body types of different persons.

Visual persons may have straight back, head looking-up, hunched shoulders, and gestures high up. They may have fingers and arms extended. Their body type may be thin, they may have a tensed body, and their skin colour may be pale.

Kinaesthetic persons may slouch or bend over. Shoulders may tend to droop. Head sits solidly on the shoulders and palms may be upturned. Kinaesthetic internal type person will have a soft body. Kinaesthetic external type person will have muscular body and will have athletic posture. Skin colour may be more colourful and redder or shiny.

Auditory person will have head on one side and may point to ears. Auditory external will lean forwards whereas auditory internal will lean back. Arms may be folded. Auditory person will tend to have body between kinaesthetic person (soft) and visual person (tense). Auditory external tends to soften whereas auditory internal tends to tighten. Skin colour of auditory person can be normal or pale.

Eye-Accessing Cues

Another cue is eye-accessing pattern. The eyes (pupils of the eyes) will move in a certain direction, indicating whether a person is constructing or remembering. Tables 8.1-8.3 show the moment of eye with reference to a person's thinking. This is for a normally organised person (majority of people). There are some reversed organised persons also.

Eye Movement	Question and Representation
	Eyes will move to up right when we construct a picture or imagine a picture. If we say, 'Propose better seating arrangement in the office space to accommodate new staff', the person will construct a picture of the office space (Visual construction).
	Eyes will move to up left when we remember a picture. If we ask, 'Which is the biggest meeting room to accommodate our team?', the team member will remember the rooms and then answer (Visual remembered).
	Sometimes, some people look straight ahead in a defocused way. This is also visualising. It may appear as a glazed look.

Table 8.1 Visual eye-accessing cues

Eye Movement	Question and Representation
	Eyes will move to side left when we remember a sound or hear word(s). If we ask, 'Who has the softest voice in our team?', the team member will recall or remember the voice and then answer (Auditory recall).
	Eyes will move to side right when we construct a sound. If we ask, 'How would you sound giving presentation in the next sales conference?', the person will construct the voice to listen (Auditory constructed).

Table 8.2 Auditory eye-accessing cues

Eye Movement	Question and Representation
	Eyes will move to downright when we are accessing touch, taste, smell, and feel. If we ask, 'What was the feeling when the audience applauded for you?', the person will access the feelings. (Kinaesthetic).
	Eyes will move to down left when we talk to ourselves, that is, internal dialogue. If we ask, 'What would you say if you win this contest?', the person will have an internal dialogue. (Auditory digital—self talk).

Table 8.3 Eye-accessing cues (Kinaesthetic and self-talk)

Breathing cue

Visual person may have shallow breathing. Breathing is high in chest. Kinaesthetic person may have deep breathing. It is low in the stomach area. Auditory person may have even breathing in the diaphragm or with the whole chest.

Voice cues

Voice cues are about tonality, tempo, and timbre. Visual persons may have fast tempo, high pitch, and nasal tonality. Kinaesthetic persons may have slow tempo with long pauses and have low and deep tonality. Auditory persons' voice may be melodic, rhythmic with clear diction. Auditory internal will have monotone, same pitch, and robot-like tonality.

8.8 Strategy (NLP Concept)

A strategy (in NLP) is a sequence of thought and behaviour based on a set of belief and sense of self to accomplish a specific outcome. It is what we do in our mind that lets us do things in our reality. In NLP terms (Refer Appendix A NLP Communication model, which shows internal representation and external behaviour), strategy is the order and sequence of internal and external representation that leads to a specific outcome.

Let us consider service transaction from a customer perspective. For example, a customer wants to buy a computer. The customer will have certain requirement specification (usage or needs) and service expectation. The customer will have a sequence of internal and external representations, and finally, the customer will buy the computer. The different strategies of the customer are as follows:

- First customer

  o Visualises laptop (Visual construction)
  o Visits the IT Mall
  o Sees the laptops at the Mall and looks at features of laptops (Visual external)

- o Self-talks to compare the requirements and available features (Auditory digital)
- o Self-talks to compare the cost and value (Auditory digital)
- o Gets information from sales person (Audio external)
- o Self-talks to select the best option. (Auditory digital)

- Second customer

  - o Remembers the description given by friend (Audio recalled)
  - o Visits the IT Mall
  - o Talks to the sales person about the interest in laptop
  - o Listens to sales person's explanation about the available laptop (Auditory external)
  - o Sees the laptops (Visual external)
  - o Asks more questions and gets more information (Auditory external)
  - o Self-talks to compare cost and value to finalise the purchase (Auditory digital)

- Third customer

  - o The customer feels the convenience in carrying the laptop (Kinaesthetic)
  - o Visits the IT Mall
  - o Sees the laptop model (Visual external)
  - o Executes commands to check software and features of the laptop (Kinaesthetic)
  - o Checks the weight and size of laptop (Kinaesthetic)
  - o Self-talks to check whether laptop is suitable for use and value for money (Auditory digital)

First customer is visual person, and his or her strategy is visual followed by auditory digital. Second customer is auditory person, and his or her strategy is auditory followed by visual and auditory digital. Third customer is kinaesthetic person, and his or her strategy is kinaesthetic followed by auditory digital.

The service provider would like to provide personalised service. This is possible when the service provider understands the customer's preferred representation system and strategy. The service provider can have strategy to sell the service. It is as follows:

- Establish rapport: Serviceperson can match physiology, tone, or words.
- Ask question: Serviceperson can ask question in the business language of the customer. This is to understand the customer and his or her—

  o Interests (Usage of laptop)
  o Values (Security, Capabilities, Entertainment, Efficiency, ease of use, reliability and so on)
  o Internal representation (Visual, Auditory, or Kinaesthetic)
  o Decision-making strategy (sequence of using different representations to arrive at the decision)
  o Convincer strategy (refer Section 11.5)
  o Reassurance strategy (reconfirmation after purchase)

- Confirm the need and value: The service person needs to check whether the customer could see value in the solution provided. This will ensure that the customer is genuine and prospect will become customer.
- Attach value to the solution: Service person emphasises on values and need and connects the laptop (product and service) with them.
- Close the sale: Service person closes the sale as the customer is satisfied with the solution. If customer has certain doubts, the salesperson can use conditional close to complete the sales.

If customer is indecisive, service person can ask questions, understand the requirement, and guide the customer with closed question to lead to the decision and develop a solution that brings value to the customer.

If customer has previous satisfactory experience with the organisation, organisation can get repeat customer. The customer shows the comfort and confidence in dealing the service provider or serviceperson.

Let us extend the example of laptop. The customer experiences a problem with the purchased laptop. He (or she) calls the service centre or visits service centre.

The above five steps are applicable. First step is to establish rapport. Second step is to ask questions to get the details of the problem. Third step is to assign the urgency and importance. This is to confirm the need and value. Fourth step is to provide solution. Value of the solution will be based on the response to the problem. If the problem is a simple issue, it must be resolved quickly. If the problem is complex, temporary solution is given quickly and permanent preventive solution is given later. The last step is to close the problem and have a satisfied customer.

In case of a problematic situation, the customer could be insistent or irate.

In the case of an insistent customer, rapport and communication are important so that the customer knows the assertive efforts and prompt proactive actions of the service provider.

In the case of an irate customer, empathy is necessary to understand the facts and feelings about the problem. The quality service and solution restores the confidence of the customer.

8.9 In Summary

Services form a significant part of businesses. Service quality depends on how the human interactions take place. Customer looks for responsiveness, promptness, and friendliness. Rapport helps to give friendly experience. If we understand customer's strategy, we can give right solution with promptness.

9

Manufacturing Management

Industrial revolution brought in manufacturing system. Quality control was soon introduced as manufactured product needs to be inspected. Information revolution has impacted manufacturing through Computer Aided Design (CAD) and Computer Aided Manufacturing (CAM). Manufacturing system became flexible manufacturing system.

Industry specific standards and practices have been developed for different industries like automobile, semiconductor, pharmaceutical and so on. Good Manufacturing Practice (GMP) gives the minimal practices to produce quality goods (refer Appendix G).

Several techniques for quality control, quality assurance, and quality management are available in manufacturing environment. Further thrust on quality can come from an innovative approach to manufacturing. From the NLP perspective, visualisation can play an important role. From the process perspective, TRIZ can provide innovation process. This chapter provides discussion on TRIZ and visualisation.

9.1 TRIZ (Theory of Inventive Problem Solving)

Innovations are keys for driving quality to the next level. An organisation can have staff suggestion scheme or brainstorming sessions to seek innovative ideas. Innovation differs from invention. Invention is transformation of thoughts into tangible idea to make up something completely new. Innovation is to introduce things to end user as if they are new.

Innovations also have certain pattern. Genrich Altshuler from patent department of Russian Navy studied nearly 200,000 patents to find

147

forty common patterns in making invention. He named the patterns as TRIZ (*teoriya resheniya izobretatelskikh zadatch*)—Russian acronym for Theory of Inventive Problem Solving. TRIZ can play an important role in designing products as well as processes in manufacturing environment. All forty patterns are listed in Appendix G.

We can consider a couple of examples. For the road works, there is a need to install traffic lights so that traffic is correctly diverted. The normal traffic light had a difficulty in transportation as well as installation. TRIZ's first principle segmentation is applied to the traffic lights, and traffic light segmented into sections with ease of assembling and disassembling. The new design for temporary usage at road works is easy and faster to install and remove.

Fifth TRIZ principle is merging or consolidation. The lawn mower is attached with the grass collector. This saved time and made ease in operation.

9.2 Visualisation

NLP communication model (refer Appendix A) shows that our experience is stored in all sensory forms, that is, visual, auditory, kinaesthetic, olfactory, and gustatory. Our mind does not distinguish between real and imaginary. We can experience through imagination. We can engage all five senses to fuel our creativity and holistic perspective. Albert Einstein said, 'Imagination is more important than knowledge. For knowledge is limited to all we know and understand, while imagination embraces the entire world and all there ever will be to know and understand.'

The word *imagination* is derived from an image, that is, a picture. Visualisation of a picture is an important part of imagination. We often tend to underrate ourselves for our visualisation capacity. However, our brain is equipped for imagination; we need to use our brain, practise visualisation, and tap our creative capabilities.

Imagination is useful for brainstorming as well as problem solving, and we can extend to visualising products and processes.

We can practice visualisation. For example, Olive Hickmott and Andrew Bendefy suggest visualising the words for spelling. Seeing spellings can help to improve the spelling ability.

9.3 Value Addition

Manufacturing converts the raw material into finished product. The value addition happens at each stage. The value addition is contributed by human beings. The following story of Birbal will help understand better.

Birbal once argued with the court poet and Akbar that man-made things can be more valuable than the natural. Birbal said he could prove his argument.

A few days later, the master craftsman presented an exquisite marble carving of a bouquet of flowers. The emperor rewarded him with 1,000 gold coins.

Just then, a small boy entered and gave Akbar a bunch of roses. Akbar thanked the boy and gave him a silver coin.

Birbal said softly, 'So the carving is more valuable than the real thing.' He proved his point. The craftsman added value to the marble stone through his carvings and made it worth 1,000 gold coins.

9.4 In Summary

As time to market is shortening, there is time pressure to design and manufacturing the products faster. Innovations are essential for creative designs and optimised manufacturing facilities. Visualisation is useful for innovations.

SECTION 5:

Maintaining quality

10

Process Management

Processes form the major chunk of quality management system (QMS). The process that manages processes is process management. This is closely linked to the Chapter 3 Quality Models and Chapter 5 QMS.

This chapter covers process maturity, process documentation, measurements and metrics, and audits and assessments.

10.1 Functions and Processes

Depending on business (that is project oriented, service oriented, manufacturing oriented or a mix of this), an organisation adopts organisational structure and common activities to form a function. Function is a team with expertise in certain area (finance, HR, Sales and so on).

Process is a set of activity with specific objective. If all activities of a process are within the function, then it is an internal process of that function. Processes can run across the functions. This is often termed as an end-to-end process.

When an organisation becomes highly function-oriented, functions often lose the organisation's vision and start working in silos.

When an organisation focuses on processes, it can integrate efforts and execute in a holistic manner.

10.2 Process Maturity

Quality Guru Philip Crosby suggested quality management maturity grid. Software companies used this concept for process improvement based on CMMI framework. COBIT Framework also adopted maturity concept for the processes. Organisation can develop their own criteria and decide maturity levels.

In Chapter 5, we have discussed 3S (System, Strategy, and Strategy). With reference to 3S, some of the maturity attributes in COBIT 4.1 are as follows:

Strategy-related attributes

- Awareness: This is about awareness of the need or requirement of process. Five levels are—

  o Level 1: Surfacing need for process
  o Level 2: Need to act on process
  o Level 3: Clear understanding on need for the process
  o Level 4: Clearly defined requirement of the process
  o Level 5: Advanced forwards looking requirements

- Policies and plans: Management needs to show clear intention. Five levels are—

  o Level 1: No policies ad-hoc approach
  o Level 2: Informal policies and plans
  o Level 3: Defined and documented policies and plans
  o Level 4: Policies and plans developed through systematic process with document control (approval and release)
  o Level 5: Integrated, end-to-end approach to policies and plans

- Goal setting and measurement: Business needs clarity on goals to achieve. Five levels are—

  o Level 1: No goal setting and no measurement
  o Level 2: Some goals are defined; some financial measure known to senior management only
  o Level 3: Some goals and measurement are set for effectiveness
  o Level 4: Some goals and measurement are set for effectiveness and efficiency and linked to business goals
  o Level 5: Integrated performance system with individual performance and process performance and focus on continual improvement; use of balanced scorecard

System-related attributes

- Communication: This is the initiative for prompt and systematic communication of the processes. Five levels are—

  o Level 1: Sporadic communication
  o Level 2: Communication in generic terms (informal)
  o Level 3: Formal and structured communication
  o Level 4: Mature communication with appropriate tools
  o Level 5: Proactive communication with right tools and techniques

- Procedures: This provides the step-by-step details of the process. Five levels are—

  o Level 1: No procedures; ad-hoc approach
  o Level 2: Informal procedures
  o Level 3: Defined and documented procedures
  o Level 4: Integrated comprehensive procedures with mechanism to have internal best practices
  o Level 5: Integrated and end-to end with external best practices (world class)

- Tools and automation: This brings efficiency to the processes. Five levels are—

  o Level 1: No plan for tool usage; some tools on individual basis
  o Level 2: Key individuals establish common approach for tool usage (informal)
  o Level 3: Plan to standardise automated tool
  o Level 4: Tools help to automate main process areas and monitor critical activities
  o Level 5: Tools are integrated with end-to-end process and automated workflow

- Skills and expertise: These are technical skills. Five levels are—

  o Level 1: Skills not identified
  o Level 2: Minimal skill requirements defined for critical job
  o Level 3: Skills defined for all jobs

o Level 4: Skills regularly updated and certification encouraged
o Level 5: Formal continual improvements of skills

- Training: These are technical trainings. Five levels are—

o Level 1: No training plan and no formal trainings
o Level 2: Ad-hoc trainings with decision by individuals and informal trainings
o Level 3: Formal training plan and formal trainings
o Level 4: In addition to formal training programme, knowledge sharing and training effectiveness assessment
o Level 5: In addition to level 4, the best practices and leading edge concepts (world class)

Synergy-related attributes

- Responsibility and accountability: Roles defined in process have the responsibilities and accountability.

o Level 1: Responsibilities and accountability are not defined
o Level 2: Some individuals assume responsibility (informal)
o Level 3: Responsibilities and accountability are defined for process
o Level 4: Process owner defined and roles with responsibilities and accountabilities are accepted
o Level 5: Process owner are empowered and acceptance of responsibilities are cascaded down throughout organisation

- Soft skills and training for soft skills: Levels are similar to the one discussed for technical skills.

Let us link system, strategy, synergy, and maturity levels with efficiency, effectiveness, and energy.

Level 1 process (initial) is chaotic. The success of a process depends on the heroics of an individual. There is lack of standard practices in an organisation, and there is no control. This can often result in blames and accusation. The system, strategy, and synergy (3Ss) will be missing. The efficiency, effectiveness, and energy (3Es) are not at all expected.

Level 2 process (repeatable) has some credibility. The processes are performed, to some extent, in a consistent manner. However, there are no process documents or training for process. Still there is a high reliance on the individuals. The system for the meetings exists with ambiguity; however, strategy and synergy are missing. The efficiency, effectiveness, and energy (3E) are not significant.

Level 3 process (defined) is standardised and documented. Tools and techniques are recommended in the process, and the process training helps to implement consistency across the organisation. There will be significant improvement in efficiency and effectiveness. Strategies are existing. However, people factor (synergy) may still be missing. There is limited monitoring or measurements. Hence, achievement of efficiency and effectiveness may not be reported.

Level 4 process (managed and measured or quantitatively managed) is a process where performance indicators are monitored. The evidence procedure is well defined, process is measured, and controls are improved. The systems are further improved for monitoring. What gets measured gets managed. Strategy will be used for better results. Executives will be aware of the importance of synergy. There is achievement of efficiency and effectiveness.

Level 5 process (optimised) is a process with system, strategy, and synergy (3S). Process will have continual improvements. Process will have creativity, innovation, and high motivation. This will have effectiveness, efficiency, and energy (3E). NLP techniques can play important role in achieving this process level.

Figure 10.1 shows the system, strategy, and synergy (3S) as inputs and efficiency, effectiveness, and energy (3E) as outputs at each process maturity level.

Process Maturity	System	Strategy	Synergy	Efficiency	Effectiveness	Energy
	Inputs			Outputs		
Level 1 (Initial)	○	○	○	○	○	○
Level 2 (Repeatable)	◐	○	○	○	○	○
Level 3 (Defined)	●	◐	○	◐	◐	○
Level 4 (Quantitatively Managed)	●	◐	◐	●	●	◐
Level 5 (Optimized)	●	●	●	●	●	●

○ Absence   ◐ Partial Presence   ● Presence

Figure 10.1 3S and 3E relationship

Expectations from people are different as process maturity improves. It is shown in Figure 10.2.

Process Maturity	Ad-hoc	Repeatable	Defined	Quantitatively Managed	Optimized
People	Heroic of People		People follow the processes		People Innovate / Optimize

Figure 10.2 People role changes with process maturity

At lower maturity level, people are busy with fire fighting. Organisations need heroes to move out of crises. At levels 3 and 4, people are expected to follow the process, and at level 4, it is management by facts. At levels 4 and 5, there are no crises, and people can devote their time in innovation and optimisation.

10.3 Process Definition

When we talk about processes, the expectation of the process user is to have documentation for the process.

ITIL recommends the following details:

- Control elements

  o Owner
  o Policy
  o Objectives
  o Feedback (Records)

- Enablers

  o Resources
  o Capabilities

- Process details

  o Trigger
  o Inputs

o Metrics
o Procedure, activities, or work instructions
o Improvement
o Output

In case of CMMI, defined process clearly states the purpose, inputs, entry criteria, activities, roles, measures, verification steps, outputs, and exit criteria.

COBIT 5 has defined the enabling processes with the following:

- Process description (in brief)
- Process purpose statement
- IT-related goals and related metrics
- Process goals and related metrics
- RACI Chart (Responsibility, Accountability, Consulted, Informed)
- Process practices, inputs/outputs and activities

An organisation should decide its own formats and define the process adequately. We can refer to ITIL, CMMI, and COBIT and bring out most suitable documentation. As discussed in Chapter 6, we need to consider various preferences of people (for example, summary form or detailed description or preference for audiovisual). The commonly used techniques for process documents are flow charts, swimlane diagram, RACI charts (Responsible, Accountable, Consulted, and informed), SIPOC (Supplier, Input, Process, Output, Customer), HIPO diagram (Hierarchy, Input, Process, Output) and so on. For example, simple meeting process is shown with swimlane diagram in Figure 10.3 and RACI chart in Figure 10.4.

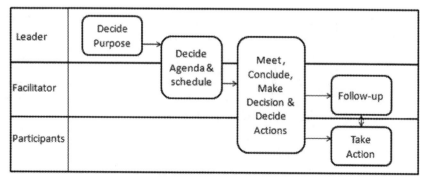

Figure 10.3 Swimlane diagram for meeting process

Process documentation is very useful for business process improvements. Another popular exercise is to prepare a Value Stream Map (VSM). This indicates value from a customer perspective of the process steps. The process will have value added activities and non-value adding activities. Maps are prepared for current workflow and analysed. With eliminating waste, map for future state are prepared. Improved process is implemented.

Activities	Leader	Facilitator	Participant(s)	Admin	Recorder/ Timer
Decide the purpose/ need for a meeting	R				
Plan the meeting/agenda	A	R			
Book the resources and block participants' calendar for the meeting	C	C	I	R	I
Distribute agenda/ information required for the meeting	A	R			
Prepare for the meeting	R	R	R		
Opening the meeting	R	R			
Discussion	A/R	R	R		
Track Time through-out meeting					R
Record notes of the meeting					R
Closing the meeting; Feedback	A	R			
Follow-up action	A	R	R		

Figure 10.4 RACI chart for meeting process

10.4 Metrics and Measurement

The nineteenth-century British Prime Minister Benjamin Disraeli once said, 'There are three kinds of lies—lies, damned lies, and statistics.' Mark Twain popularised the term further. The following story of Akbar and Birbal illustrates it.

One day, Akbar and Birbal were taking a walk in the palace gardens. While watching the crows, a question popped in Akbar's mind. He asked, 'Birbal, how many crows are there in my kingdom?'

After a moment's thought, Birbal replied, 'Your Majesty, there are 95,563 crows in the kingdom.'

Amazed by his quick response, Akbar tried to test him again by asking, 'If there are more crows than you mentioned?'

Without any hesitation, Birbal replied, 'Your Majesty, it means some crows are visiting from neighbouring kingdoms. And if there is less number of crows than I mentioned, it means some crows from our kingdom may have gone on holidays to other places.'

Birbal showed how numbers and statistics can be manipulated.

In today's business, some people try to manage numbers. Birbal has shown that numbers and statistics are vulnerable unless we receive from proper process or system.

When we discussed that goal should be measurable or when we talked maturity level 4 quantitatively managed, the emphasis should be on how the numbers are achieved than what the numbers are achieved.

We need to set up measurement system to have reliable reporting of metrics. This includes source of obtaining data, data collection, analysis, and reporting. Books on quality assurance have covered measurement and analysis with in-depth discussion on statistical tools.

From the NLP perspective, measurement system needs to be linked to the SMART goals as well as motivation.

We discussed Balanced Scorecard briefly in Chapter 3. Balance Scorecard can be used for quality programme. Four parameters are as follows:

- Financial: General strategy is investing in quality assurance and quality control so that failure cost is reduced significantly. Quality costs are broadly divided into three categories:

  o Failure cost: Cost associated with defects and repair.

o Appraisal cost: Cost associated with quality control (i.e., inspections, reviews, and testing)

o Preventive cost: Cost associated with QMS development, trainings, and process improvements.

- Customer: Employees, customers, and suppliers are users of the QMS. Employees' satisfaction about the QMS is important.
- Operational parameter: This should consider the efficiencies of key processes.
- Learning and development: This represents learning and development activities (discussed in Chapter 6) and indicates the skills and capabilities built for the business.

10.5 Four Stages of Competence

Processes define roles and responsibilities. People need competencies to take the responsibilities. The competencies progresses in stages. Table 10.1 shows the four stages.

Conscious	(2)We do know what we don't know	(3)We know what we know
Unconscious	(1)We don't know what we don't know	(4)We don't know what we know
	Incompetence	Competence

Table 10.1 Four stages of competence

Let us consider IT department introducing problem management process.

Before the introduction of problem management process, we do not know that we do not know some of the problem-solving technique; for example, Kepner Treoge technique for problem solving. This is unconscious incompetence.

When problem management process is introduced, we know that we do not know some of the problem-solving techniques. This is conscious incompetence.

As a part of rolling out problem management process, trainings on problem solving are conducted. We learn new problem-solving techniques. We use those techniques in solving problems. We need to pay attention consciously to the steps in the problem-solving technique. This is conscious competence.

As we repeat practicing the steps of problem solving, the steps move to our unconscious. When we perform problem solving, the steps are taken unconsciously (or unknowingly), and we become an expert in problem solving. This is unconscious competence.

Process compliance becomes natural when a person achieves unconscious competence. For example, people prefer a surgeon with experience because there is an assumption that a surgeon has the unconscious competence to perform the operations well. From a quality person perspective, the surgeon takes care of all processes of the operation to deliver a quality service.

10.6 Process Evaluation

Processes are monitored through measurement and metrics reporting at planned intervals. Other exercise is evaluation. Evaluation is done through reviews or audits. ISO 9000 has a clause for internal audit under monitoring and measurement. As per ISO 19011 standard, audit is defined as follows:

Systematic, independent, and documented process of obtaining audit evidence (i.e., records, statement of facts, or information) and evaluating it objectively to determine the extent to which the audit criteria (requirement of standard, policies, or process) are fulfilled. If there is a lack of evidence, non-conformity is reported.

When we ask people, 'Do you like audits?' or, 'Are you excited to meet the auditor?', the usual answer is, 'No, we do not like to get audited'. Audit is mostly discouraging. In some organisations, it becomes a routine to have audits, raise the non-conformances, and close the non-conformances. In such a situation, management may question the benefits of quality programme.

There are several books on quality audits. To make audit programme attractive, the following points are useful:

- Auditor should understand the model of the world of people getting audited. This will reduce the miscommunication.
- Unconscious mind takes everything personally. Audit findings are shown as issues with quality management system; however, people take as their own mistakes and even feel guilty about it.

- Auditor should appreciate the positive findings in the audit report.
- While introducing process and QMS, we need to make people aware of the need for control and records. People think controls as obstacles in work and then ignore the controls. This will result in non-conformance. Awareness about control and records is necessary.

10.7 In Summary

Process management forms the backbone of quality management system. Continual improvement is essentially process improvements. Process improvements can happen three ways:

- Maturity assessment of process and plan to improve maturity
- Value stream map to assess how value addition takes place
- Monitoring through metrics reporting and evaluating, using reviews and audits

The motivation of people is important for process improvements, and people will make the essential difference through their competencies.

11

Change Management

Business dynamic is leading to constant changes. Organisations need to have a strategy for change management. Several researchers have worked on change management and developed models for change. These models provide excellent summary of how organisation can adopt change.

This chapter first gives existing models and then provides NLP aspects for change management.

11.1 ADKAR Model (Awareness, Desire, Knowledge, Ability, Reinforcement)

Prosci (ref www.change-management.com) first published ADKAR model in 1998, and Jeff Hiat's book on ADKAR was published in 2006. ADKAR model gives the changes for people with reference to the project phases.

- Business need phase: Awareness of the need to change; know the reasons and risks of not changing
- Project definition phase: Desire to support the change and participate in the project
- Design and solution development phase: Knowledge about the change and details of what to do
- Implementation phase: Ability to implement the change and use the new system in day-to-day life on a day-to-day basis.
- Post-implementation phase: Reinforcement to sustain the change. Use reward and recognition.

Propsi's change management learning centre provides more details on how to build awareness, create desire, develop knowledge, foster ability, and reinforce the change.

11.2 Kotter's Theory

John Kotter (reference www.kotterinternational.com) developed eight steps process to lead the change. The eight steps are—

- Creating sense of urgency: Leaders need to understand current state of organisation—'No urgency' or 'False urgency' or 'True urgency'. 'No urgency' means the people in the organisation do not have action and result. 'False urgency' means people have action without result. 'True urgency' means people are looking for action with results. This step also looks for appeal to the heart with inspiration than just logical appeal to the head. Creating a sense of urgency means having true urgency with a hearty appeal.
- Forming a guiding coalition: Four essential qualities are position power (authority), expertise (intelligent decision-making), credibility (respected stature), and leadership (passion to drive). A team with these four qualities can have the capacity of making a change reality.
- Creating a change vision: Effective vision can be developed based on six parameters—imaginable (clear picture of future), feasible (realistic goal), focused (clear purpose), flexibility (options for achieving), desirable (long-term interest), and communicable (easily stated). It serves as guide for decision and as glue with motivation and coordination.
- Communicating the vision: Consistently communicate to all through interesting, interactive, and positive way. Use of analogy and stories and walk the talk will be effective.
- Empowering others to act on the vision: There will be barriers because of (rigid) organisation structure or (rigid) people. This requires internal restructuring for change and honest dialogue to eliminate the barriers, and let the best come out of the change.
- Planning for and creating quick wins: Short-term wins need to be incorporated so that sense of urgency will be enforced. Change becomes visible and viable.

- Consolidating improvements and producing more change:
- Institutionalise the change: This is the sustainability and cultural change. Promote behavioural norms and shared values.

Kotter International provides the detailed eight-step approach. John Kotter also has a book *Leading Change* on the same subject.

11.3 Lewin Change Model

Kurt Lewin presented change model way back in 1947. It has three stages—Unfreeze, Change (transform), and Freeze.

Unfreeze stage explores reason for change supported by data (facts)— poor financial results or decrease in sales or in customer satisfaction. This requires relooking at behaviour, beliefs, values, and attitude. This will create uncertainty as decision to change is taken with all pros and cons.

Change stage is a transformation process. This stage needs communication about the desired stage. This may use role models and requires time for learning the desired stage.

Freeze stage requires trainings and support. This is to sustain the change and effectively make cultural change.

11.4 Satir Change Model

Virginia Satir developed a five-stage model for change. This is impact-based model and impact is with reference to the people. We have seen continual improvement PDCA cycle in Chapter 4, Section 4.1. Under ideal condition, continual improvement is as shown in Figure 11.1. With Satir change model, realistic improvement progress is as shown in Figure 11.2.

Stage 1—Late status quo: People are in comfort zone. They are familiar with processes and standards. Late status quo is shown as current baseline (quality term). Even if there are issues, they know who to approach and how to resolve.

Stage 2—Resistance: We start preparing plan (P) for improvements. This will be a foreign element for (some of) the people, and people start resisting the change. There can be a drop in performance, and quality suffers. Leaders need to make them aware of change and handle the reaction in a subtle way. Communication plays key role in handling the resistance.

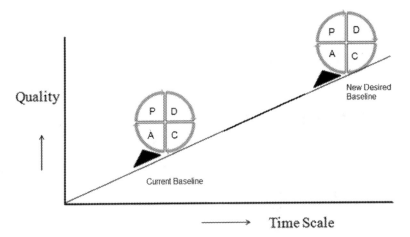

Figure 11.1 Continual improvement PDCA cycle in ideal situation

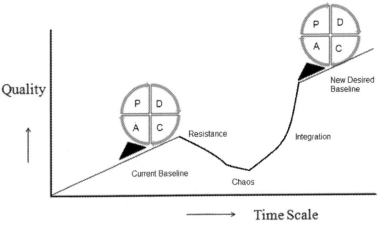

Figure 11.2 Continual improvement PDCA cycle
with Satire change model stages

Stage 3—Chaos: After the plan, it is 'Do' phase. People are not clear about the new role, new processes, and new standards. They are clear about what is expected of them. This becomes a chaotic situation. Quality and performance reaches rock bottom. This happens till the people accept the new process as planned (the foreign element).

Stage 4—Integration: After the 'Do' phase, it is 'Check' phase. Check means looking at data and analysing the situation. This will give inputs to the desired state. Transforming ideas are suggested to resolve issues. This stage needs greater support so that teams can come out chaos and have integrated approach to resolve various issues.

Stage 5—New status quo: After the 'check' phase, it is 'Act' phase. The corrective actions take the performance to a new level. There is a sense of achievement. This forms a new baseline.

11.5 NLP Aspects for Change

Neurological levels and meta programmes are discussed in this section. Ways of changing beliefs are in the subsequent sections.

Neurological levels

We have discussed this in Chapter 5. We need to check at what level the change is taking place. All level below that level will be impacted. Hence, it is essential to determine the highest level where the change is taking place. In case of problem solving, the change should take place at least one level higher. Once correct level is determined, the change and its impact can be analysed and planned.

People's choice for communication

Communication is an important element in change management. All models discussed earlier in this chapter have stressed the importance of communication at every stage of change.

In Chapter 6, we have discussed people's preference as VAK (Visual, Auditory, kinaesthetic). This is applicable to convincing people for change. The answer to the question 'how do you know new initiative (change) is taken?' varies with people:

- I have seen it—These are visual persons. When they see presentations, physical object (new equipment), or progress charts, they are convinced about new initiative.
- I heard about it—These are auditory persons. When they hear formally or informally, they are certain about the change.

- I read about it—These are auditory digital persons, who do self-talk. When they read formal email or memo or notice, they are sure about the change.
- I am working on it—These are kinaesthetic persons. Action speaks louder than the words. When they are involved in work, they are convinced about the change.

Another aspect of convincing people is frequency of communication. This varies from person to person.

- Automatic: These people are convinced with the first communication.
- Number of times: These people need communication multiple times. This can be done by giving different examples or by reporting data. They will be satisfied with a certain number.
- Period of time: These people need time to gather information and understand the details. These people are convinced over the period of time. Leaders need to wait.
- Consistent: These people need consistent communication and are most difficult to convince. They will accept with resistance. Leaders need to work all the methods to communicate them.

Communication should take care of method and frequency to reach out to everyone in the organisation affected by the change.

11.6 Changing Belief

We discussed the importance of beliefs in Chapter 4 as well as in Chapter 5. NLP practitioner and master practitioner courses teach ways to change internal representation (in our mind) and, subsequently, change our belief. This exercise must be done under supervision.

In NLP, an anchor means trigger or stimulus to a specific state of mind. We will use anchors to erase limiting belief and install desired belief. For example, in this case, an executive or client is graduate engineer, and he thinks he is not good at English. His limiting belief is 'I am not good at English'. Due to his limiting belief, he does not speak in a meeting or has lack of confidence to speak to his seniors. This affects his performance, and the organisation also loses proper contribution from the employee. We will walk through exercise that will change this limiting belief.

For this exercise, we mark 4 squares on the floor as shown in figure 11.3. Square 1 and 2 are close enough. Similarly, step 3 and 4 are close enough. Four steps represent 4 different beliefs.

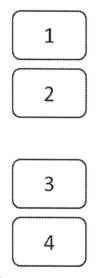

Figure 11.3 Four squares represent four steps

Square 1 represents the limiting belief (first belief). For example, I am not good at English.

Square 2 represents the belief which is no longer true (Second belief). As a child, you may be believing it and then as a grown-up person, you realise it is not true. For example, Santa Clause brings gifts for you.

Square 3 represents the desired or empowering belief (Third belief). For example, I have confidence to speak in English. This is done by visualizing event when I spoke English confidently or visualize desired state.

Square 4 represents the belief that is known as true (Fourth belief). For example, the square has 4 sides or the tennis ball is round.

The first four steps are anchored for beliefs and then limiting belief is erased and new empowering belief is installed. NLP Practitioner (or master practitioner) instructs the following steps:

- Step on square 1 and experience the limiting belief. For example, I am not good at English.
- Step back from square 1 and break the state (by asking questions like 'What's the time?').
- Step on square 2 and experience the belief which is no longer true. For example, Santa Clause brings gifts for you

- Step back from square 2 and break the state (by asking colour of a wall).
- Step on square 3 and experience the empowering belief. For example, I am good at English.
- Step back from square 3 and break the state. (by asking questions like 'What's the time?').
- Step on square 4 and experience the known true belief. For example, the tennis ball is round.
- Step back from square 4 and break the state. (by asking colour of a wall)
- Move near squares 1 and 2.
- Step right leg on square 1, and after experiencing limiting belief, put left leg on square 2 (that is to stand on both squares 1 and 2). This triggers second belief.
- Move out and break the state.
- Move near squares 3 and 4
- Step right leg on square 3, and after experiencing third belief, put left leg on square 4 (to stand on both squares 3 and 4). This triggers fourth belief.
- Move out and break the state.
- Test for belief three, that is the empowering or desired belief.

We can use similar method for changing values.

11.7 Sleight of Mouth

Sleight of mouth is magic that works with language. This is used for reframing the statement (belief). There are sixteen patterns to reframe. The following example will illustrate the sleight of mouth.

Statement: 'Quality means documentation'.

- Pattern 1 (metaframe on whole equivalence): You are just thinking that way because your view narrowed down to documentation and unrealistic expectation through documentation.
- Pattern 2 (reality strategy on cause/evidence): How do you know documentation is synonym for quality?

- Pattern 3 (model of the world on cause/evidence): Most people judge quality based on their experience with product or service not based on documents.
- Pattern 4 (apply to self on—cause/evidence): This is a common belief among many. It would be interesting when many people understand quality beyond documentation.
- Pattern 5 (apply to self on belief/value/effect): Are you sure documentation takes care of all aspects of quality?
- Pattern 6 (Change frame [size, context] on cause/evidence): Is this a belief which the whole organisation needs to have?
- Pattern 7 (hierarchy of criteria on effect/belief/value): Don't you think satisfaction of different stakeholders as a part of quality product/service is important than documentation?
- Pattern 8 (Consequence): By equating quality with documentation and focusing on documentation, it will lead to documentation overhead and bureaucracy.
- Pattern 9 (Another outcome): The real quality is all about excellence.
- Pattern 10 (Metaphor/analogy on effect/belief/value): The sweets are nicely packed; however, they taste horrible. Can we equate nice packing with taste?
- Pattern 11 (Redefine on cause/evidence): Documentation is part of quality as per requirement.
- Pattern 12 (Redefine on effect/values/belief): Documentation may help in some aspects of quality.
- Pattern 13 (Chunk down on effect/belief/value): How specifically meets different aspects of quality.
- Pattern 14 (Chunk up [exaggerate] on cause/evidence): This means the most important aspect of business is documentation.
- Pattern 15 (Counter example on cause/evidence): Is it possible that there is a documentation and yet quality is not good?
- Pattern 16 (intent on cause/evidence) Intention is not to intimidate documentation; it is giving bigger picture of quality.

More can be learned in NLP Master Practitioner course about sleight of mouth.

11.8 Change Management Process

Organisation needs to have change management process. ADKAR model has communication and project alignment. Kotter's model starts with vision and hence very useful for large organisational change. The Lewin model gives excellent analogy, and the Satir model considers people factor.

For developing change management process, we need to consider all factors discussed in various models and develop the best-suited process for the organisation. Process can make use of NLP tools discussed in this chapter. Process should be flexible to handle changes at different levels.

11.9 In Summary

Change management needs system, strategy, and synergy. Changes can happen at any neurological level. If correct neurological level is not determined for change, then change management will go for a toss. Change management process and tools provide the system. Careful planning of different aspects will bring strategy. People management and communication will address the synergy.

APPENDICES

APPENDIX A

NLP Communication Model

NLP Communication model is studied in detail in NLP course. Here is a brief description.

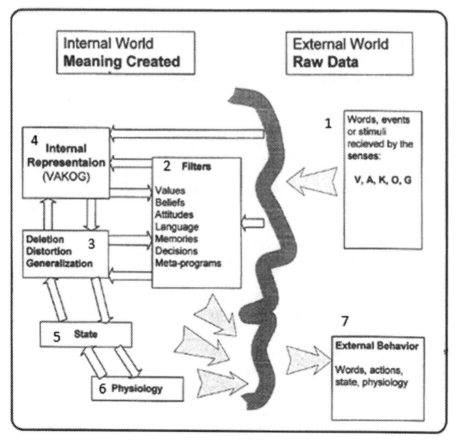

Source: NLP Practitioner Work Book.

1. External stimulus: Acronym VAKOG is based on our five senses:

   (a) Vision—what we see
   (b) Auditory—what we hear
   (c) Kinaesthetic—what we feel
   (d) Olfactory—what we smell
   (e) Gustatory—what we taste

2. Filters: The information goes through filters like values and beliefs, Meta programmes and so on. This will have an impact on information.

3. Deletion, Distortion, Generalisation: These three filters impact the inputs. Deletion happens as we pay attention to the inputs selectively, Distortion happens when we modify those inputs, and Generalisation happens when we put information under certain category or classification. For example, a purchase manager asked a purchase officer, 'What is the status of purchase order number N to the vendor ABC?' The purchase officer answered, 'I reminded ABC two days back, delivery may be delayed by two to three days.' The director asked the same question to the purchase manager, for which the purchase manager answered, 'As usual, ABC will delay by week.' The purchase manager deleted information about reminder, distorted the number of days for the delay, and, by using 'as usual', indicated generalisation.

4. Internal Representation: This is an experience stored in our memory. It is in the form VAKOG, meaning, all five senses. For example, someone has a playful Pomeranian dog as a pet. Someone else had dog bite and had to take painful injections. When we say 'dog', both will have different internal representation because of their experience. Hence, we say everyone is unique and everyone has a unique model of the world.

5. State: State of mind means mood or feelings

6. Physiology: We agree that body and mind are connected. Richard Bandler says body and mind are connected through language or self-talk. Our body speaks the same language as our thoughts or feelings and vice versa is also true. Adopt physiology of happy state, and you will find it difficult to think of sad state.

7. External behaviour: The behaviour observed by other persons.

APPENDIX B

NLP Presuppositions

1. Everyone has a unique **model of the world.**
2. Respect the other person's **model of the world.**
3. People are **map** makers.
4. People's **maps** are made of pictures, sounds, feelings, smells, and tastes (VAKOG—Visual, Auditory, Kinaesthetic, Olfactory, and Gustatory).
5. People respond to their **maps** of reality, not to reality itself
6. The **map** is not the territory.
7. If you change your **map,** you will change your emotional state.
8. Behind every **behaviour** is a positive intention.
9. People are not their **behaviours.**
10. The meaning of the **behaviour** is dependent on the context it is exhibited.
11. All **behaviour** has positive intention.
12. The most important thing about a person is that person's **behaviour.**
13. Every **behaviour** is useful in some context.
14. The positive worth of an individual is held constant, while the value and appropriateness of internal and or external **behaviour** is questioned.
15. The person with the most **flexibility** in his or her **behaviours** will have greater influence over others.
16. **Choice** is better than no choice.
17. People always make the best **choices** available to them.
18. All procedures should be designed to create **choice** and promote wholeness.
19. Everyone is doing the best they can with the **resources** they have available.

20. There are no un-**resource**ful people, only un-resourceful states.
21. Everyone is in charge of their mind and, therefore, their **results**.
22. People work perfectly to produce the **results** they get.
23. If one person can do something, anyone can **learn** to do it.
24. People already have all the **resources** they need to achieve their desired outcomes.
25. There is no such thing as failure, only **feedback**.
26. **Experience** has a structure.
27. If what you are doing is not working, **do something else**.
28. Positive **change** always comes from adding resources.
29. The mind and body are parts of the same **system** and affect each other.
30. The most flexible element in any **system** can control the system.
31. The meaning of the **communication** is the response you get.
32. Resistance in a client (other person) is a lack of **rapport**.
33. The quality of our lives is determined by the quality of our **communication**.
34. There is no substitute for clean, open **sensory channels**.

APPENDIX C

Meta Programmes

In Appendix A, there is communication model, and it shows a list of filters in Box 2. One of the filters is meta programme. There are several meta programmes that operate and influence us. More about meta programmes can be studied at NLP Master practitioner level. Some of them are discussed in various chapters. To get an idea on how a person thinks and acts differently, here are a few meta programmes with two polarities:

Direction filter (Away and Towards)

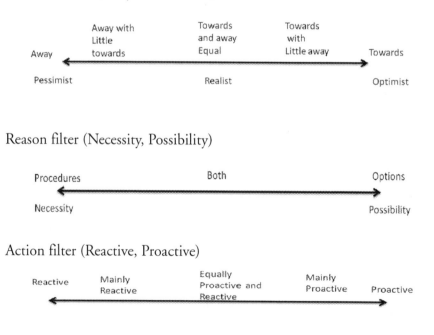

Reason filter (Necessity, Possibility)

Action filter (Reactive, Proactive)

Judging results (External, Internal)

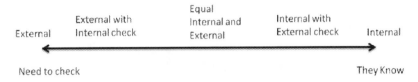

Paying attention (Self, Others)

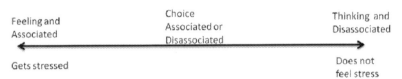

Dealing with stress (Associated, Disassociated)

Feeling and Associated	Choice Associated or Disassociated	Thinking and Disassociated
Gets stressed		Does not feel stress

Chunk size (Details, Big picture)

Details	Details then big picture	Big picture then details	Big picture
Specific			Abstract

APPENDIX D

Managing and Leading Quality

We often use the term total quality management (TQM). It focuses on management. However, for supercharged quality, there is a need to lead quality as well as manage quality. We need managers as well as leaders.

Leaders will set the direction through vision and mission. Leaders provide the strategic direction. Managers are good at preparing plans and executing them in an efficient manner.

Leaders build teams and motivate them. Leaders provide trainings and coach or mentor people. Managers are good at organising and solving problems and ensure necessary controls in the execution.

Leaders have questioning ability to challenge current practices and act as a change agent. Managers are good in implementing and setting up rules and regulations and enforcing them.

Leaders focus on ideas and innovations; managers look at status reporting and maintaining status quo.

APPENDIX E

Risk Management

Business or product or project is seen from a risk perspective. Risk management is essentially predicting the obstacle in the plans and being prepared to handle those obstacles. It is a forwards-looking process. CMMI, COBIT, ITIL, and project management frameworks (PMBOK) have risk management process. Other processes like business continuity, security management, and product testing also have risk management embedded in them. We can consider from strategy, system, and synergy perspectives.

- Strategy: Senior management defines policy on investments on projects by minimising the risk and maximising the returns. Management also defines policy on monitoring risks, considering the source of risk, risk identification, risk mitigation, and contingency plans.
- System: This defines the processes linked with risk and records to be necessary for ongoing monitoring of risk. General steps can be as follows:

  o Identify risks, their impact, and likelihood
  o Evaluate, categorise, and prioritise risks
  o Develop risk management plan
  o Get approval and get funding for risk management plan
  o Monitor risks and maintain risk management plan

- Synergy: There are two polarities: risk-averse and risk-prone. The team needs to reach consensus on optimisation of risks, synergy, or teamwork in business continuity.

APPENDIX F

ISO 9001 QMS

ISO 9001 Quality Management System is a most commonly used standard. The standard provides the requirements. Quality professionals are aware of requirements, whereas others can look at clauses; the clauses are as follows:

- Quality Management System

    o General requirements
    o Documentation requirement

        - General
        - Quality manual
        - Control of documents
        - Control of records

- Management responsibility

    o Management commitment
    o Customer focus
    o Quality policy
    o Planning

        - Quality objective
        - Quality Management System Planning

    o Responsibility, authority, and communication

- Responsibility and authority
- Management representative
- Internal communication

o Management review

- General
- Review input
- Review output

- Resource management

  o Provision of resources
  o Human resources

  - General
  - Competence, training, and awareness

  o Infrastructure
  o Work environment

- Product realisation

  o Planning of product realisation
  o Customer-related processes

  - Determination of requirements related to the product
  - Review of requirements related to the product
  - Customer communication

  o Design and development

  - Design and development planning
  - Design and development inputs
  - Design and development outputs
  - Design and development review

- Design and development verification
- Design and development validation
- Control of design and development changes

- Purchasing

  - Purchasing process
  - Purchasing information
  - Verification of purchased product

- Production and service provision

  - Control of production and service provision
  - Validation of processes for production and service provision
  - Identification and traceability
  - Customer property
  - Preservation of product

- Controlling of monitoring and measuring equipment

- Measurement, analysis, and improvement

  - General
  - Monitoring and measurement

    - Customer satisfaction
    - Internal audit
    - Monitoring and measurement of processes
    - Monitoring and measurement of products

  - Control of non-conforming products
  - Analysis of data
  - Improvement

    - Continual improvement
    - Corrective action
    - Preventive action

APPENDIX G

Good Manufacturing Practice

Good Manufacturing Product (GMP) is a set of regulations, codes, and guidelines for the manufacture of food, drug, and medical devices. This is a closely linked quality. The quality of these products has direct impact on health. Countries (as well as the World Health Organisation) have regulations or guidelines for GMP. Major categories of GMP are as follows:

- Sale
- Premises
- Equipment
- Personnel
- Sanitation
- Raw material testing
- Manufacturing control
- Quality control department
- Packaging material testing
- Finished product testing
- Records
- Samples
- Stability
- Sterile product
- Medical gases

APPENDIX H

TRIZ

TRIZ (Theory of Inventive Problem Solving) provides forty patterns. The details can be seen at www.triz-journal.com (and many other websites on TRIZ). To have an idea, the forty principles of TRIZ are as follows:

- Segmentation
- Taking out
- Local quality
- Asymmetry
- Merging
- Universality
- Nested doll
- Anti-weight
- Preliminary anti-action
- Preliminary action
- Beforehand cushioning
- Equipotentiality
- The other way round
- Spheroidality—Curvature
- Dynamics
- Partial or excessive actions
- Another dimension
- Mechanical vibration
- Periodic action
- Continuity of useful action
- Skipping
- Blessing in disguise or 'Turn Lemons into Lemonade'
- Feedback
- Intermediary

- Self-service
- Copying
- Cheap short-living objects
- Mechanics substitution
- Pneumatics and hydraulics
- Flexible shells and thin films
- Porous materials
- Colour changes
- Homogeneity
- Discarding and recovering
- Parameter changes
- Phase transitions
- Thermal expansion
- Strong oxidants
- Inert atmosphere
- Composite materials

APPENDIX I

QC Tools

'Seven QC tools' is a popular term in quality management. These tools are most commonly used for improvements. Many tools are based on statistics. Books on quality provide detailed discussion. Quality professionals know and use these tools. For others, it is good to be aware. The tools are as follows:

- Cause and effect diagram: This is to explore and arrange the list of causes of the undesirable effect. The team can brainstorm and then construct cause and effect diagram. This is also known as Ishikawa diagram or Fish-bone diagram.
- Pareto analysis: This is also known as 80:20 rule—20 per cent causes have 80 per cent effect. This is to find the vital few and drop trivial many.
- Histogram: This is a frequency distribution chart. This simple statistical tool is used to find the type of distribution.
- Scatter diagram: This is used to find the correlation of two variables. When there is correlation, linearity is observed in the diagram.
- Control charts: These are used to check whether the process is in statistical control. The variation in process is linked to process capability. The details of different control charts are available in Statistical Quality Control books.
- Check sheet: This is a list of common defects. It is used to collect data on defects.
- Flow chart: This is a graphical representation of process.

Quality professionals have added another set of seven QC tools. These are known as 'New Seven QC Tools'. These are as follows

- Relations diagram: This is a visual representation of interrelationship between the causes in complex problems.
- Affinity diagram: This is a visual representation of large number of ideas in logical groups.
- Tree diagram: This is a visual representation of full range of paths with tasks in sequential order to achieve desired objective.
- Arrow diagram: This is a network diagram for project planning, scheduling and monitoring.
- Matrix diagram: This is two dimensional table (column and row) to define the existence and the extent of relationship between two sets of information
- Matrix data: This is a matrix with relationship between two sets expressed quantitatively.
- Process decision programme chart: This is a visual chart that is used to analyse the obstacles and required counter-measures.

BIBLIOGRAPHY

- *NLP Practitioner Work Book*, compiled, written, and edited by David J. Lincoln, ANLP India (2012).
- *Master Practitioner of NLP*, compiled, written, and edited by David J. Lincoln, ANLP India (2012).
- *NLP Trainers Training*, compiled and edited by David J. Lincoln, ANLP India (2012).
- *NLP for Curious*, David J. Lincoln, ANLP India (2012).
- *NLP at Work: The Difference that Makes the Difference in Business*, Sue Knight, Nicholas Brealey, London (2nd edn., 2002).
- *Modeling with NLP*, Robert Dilts, Meta Publication, Capitola, CA (1998).
- *Words That Change Minds: Mastering the Language of Influence*, Shelle Rose Charvet, Success Strategy, Kendall/Hunt Publishing, Dubuque, IA (1997).
- *Live Your Dream: Let Reality Catch-Up*, Roger Ellerton, Trafford Publishing, Bloomington, IN (2006).
- *Countermove: A Guide to the Art of Negotiation*, Ralph Watson, published by Ralph Watson (2009).
- *Seeing Spells Achieving*, Olive Hickmott and Andrew Bendefy, MX Publishing, London (2006).
- *Online Therapy: Reading between the Lines*, Jethro Adlington, MX Publishing, London (2009).
- *Mind with a Heart*, Richard P. McHugh, Gujarat Sahitya Prakash, Anand, India (6th edn., 2009).
- *Awaken the Giant Within: How to take the Immediate Control of your Mental, Emotional, Physical and Financial Destiny*, Anthony Robbins, Simon and Schuster (1997).
- *The Magic of Thinking Big: Set Your Goals High . . . Then Exceed Them,* David J. Schwartz, Pocket Books (2006).
- *Managers Who Make a Difference: Sharpening Your Management Skills,* T.V. Rao, IIM Ahamadabad Business Book, Random House India (2010).

- *Solve Your Problems: The Birbal Way,* Anita S.R. Vas and Luis S.R. Vas, Pustak Mahal, New Delhi. (2002)
- *Guide to the Common Body of Knowledge for Certified Software Quality Assurance Analyst,* Quality Assurance Institute, USA (2006).
- *CMMI for Acquisition,* Version 1.3, Software Engineering Institute, Carnegie Mellon University (2010).
- *CMMI for Development,* Version 1.3, Software Engineering Institute, Carnegie Mellon University (2010).
- *CMMI for Service,* Version 1.3, Software Engineering Institute, Carnegie Mellon University (2010).
- *COBIT 4.1,* IT Governance Institute, USA (2007).
- *COBIT 5.0,* ISACA, USA (2012).
- *ISO 9001 Quality Management System—Requirements,* ISO (2008).
- *ISO 9000 Quality Management System—Fundamentals and Vocabulary,* ISO (2005).
- *ISO 20000 Information technology—Service management Part 1 Specification, ISO (2005)*
- *Quality Tale,* National Productivity Board, Singapore (1993)
- *Put your passion into action,* Ralph Watson, published by Ralph Watson (2012)
- *Think Like an Entrepreneur,* Robbie Steinhouse and Chris West, Pearson Education Limited, Upper Saddle River, NJ (2008).
- *Brilliant Decision Making,* Robbie Steinhouse, Pearson Education Limited, Upper Saddle River, NJ (2010).
- *Toastmasters' The Leadership Excellence Series,* Toastmaster International, Mission Viejo CA 92690 USA (2010)
- *Toastmasters' High Performance Leadership,* Toastmaster International, Mission Viejo CA 92690 USA (2009)
- *ITIL Training,* Accredited course material provided by Purple Griffon Ltd, UK (2009)
- *Agile Project Management White paper,* DSDM Consortium and APMG International, (2011)
- *Service quality models: a review,* Nitin Seth, S G Deshmukh (IIT Delhi) and Prem Vrat (IIT Roorkee), International Journal of Quality & Reliability Management, Vol.22, No. 9, 2005
- *NLP For tester—The Meta Model,* Alan Richardson, Compendium Developments, UK (2004)
- *Winning with software: An executive Strategy,* Watts S Humphrey, Addison-Wesley (2002)

- *The 7 Habits of Highly Effective People.* Stephen Covey, Pocket Book, New York (2004)
- *Switched-On Quality: How to tap into the energy needed for fuller and deeper buyin,* John Guaspari, Paton Press(2002)

Websites

- www.change-management-coach.com
- www.change-management.com
- www.mindtools.com
- www.satirworkshops.com
- www.stevenmsmith.com
- www.toastmasters.org
- www.itcportal.com
- www.itil-officialsite.com
- geert-hofstede.com
- www.pmi.org
- www.prince2.com
- www.wilsonlearning.eu
- www.triz-journal.com
- www.funderstanding.com
- www.wikipedia.com

INDEX